Dear Fairing and Lucy,

please know Jon Francis, an amazing young man, who once lived joyfully and loved boldly,

BRINGING JON HOME

Peace,

David Francis

Bringing Jon Home

The Wilderness Search for Jon Francis

David Francis

Foreword by Patty Wetterling

ISBN 13: 978-1-59298-327-8

Library of Congress Control Number: 2010923342

Printed in the United States of America
First Printing: 2010
14   13   12   11   10   5   4   3   2   1

Book design by Ryan Scheife, Mayfly Design (www.mayflydesign.net)

BEAVER'S POND
PRESS

Beaver's Pond Press, Inc.
7104 Ohms Lane, Suite 101
Edina, MN 55439-2129
(952) 829-8818
www.BeaversPondPress.com

To order, visit www.BeaversPondBooks.com
or call (800) 901-3480. Reseller discounts available.

This book is dedicated to Linda, my life partner, wife, and mother of Jon;
you bore for us a remarkable son.

and

in memory of
Jonathan David Francis
(1982-2006)

CONTENTS

FOREWORD

I was devastated when I heard that Jon Francis was missing.

I knew a lot about missing children, the response needed, how to work with law enforcement, how to engage the media. I had learned these things after my son Jacob was kidnapped and our family worked with so many—way too many—other searching families. But Jon's disappearance was different. As much as I wanted to help, I knew little about finding a missing adult on a mountain.

David brilliantly captures the many stages of the search, of his family's grief, and of their process of remembering. If there was a person or a resource to help anywhere, this amazing family found it and now offers that knowledge to others.

The world lost an amazing person on the Grand Mogul; but no mountain, no person, and no accident can take away Jon's spirit and love—and the energy that he poured into his life. We can all carry those things forward in our own lives with those we care about.

This is an amazing story of love and commitment, honoring the promise that we make to our children: *I'll always be here for you.* They did it. They brought Jon home.

I wish I had met Jon. This book allowed me to meet him and live my life a little deeper because of knowing him. Thank you, David.

Patty Wetterling
Children's Safety Advocate
Jacob Wetterling Resource Center
www.jwrc.org

INTRODUCTION

Jon Francis was twenty-four years old when he climbed the 9,733-foot Grand Mogul in the Sawtooth Mountain Range in Central Idaho on July 15, 2006. In the blink of an eye, in the slip of a foot, he vanished.

After a hasty and incomplete search the sheriff's deputy said to me, "David, you need to give your son up to the mountain." Since neither local, state, nor federal agencies would continue the search for our son, the Francis family organized, funded, and joined together to carry out a massive search for Jon. The unprecedented effort attracted national attention in the search and rescue community.

While searching for my son, I learned much more about him. In my mind at the time, Jon was still my little boy, who needed to be reminded to pick up his clothes and to put gas in the tank. But to countless others we met in the days, months, and now years, that followed, there was a Jon who I came to know as a remarkable young man who led an inspiring life.

Chapter 1

THE GRAND MOGUL

Sunday, July 16, 2006, Stillwater, Minnesota

The first summer after my retirement I was enjoying the fruits of my labor, an empty nest, and more time with Linda, my wife and loving partner of forty-four years. On this sunny afternoon, having taken a day off from my campaign for the Minnesota State Senate, I was playing Monopoly with my ten-year-old granddaughter, Katie, when the phone rang. Seeing "Luther Heights" on the Caller ID, I felt a wave of happiness that our son Jon was calling home from the Bible camp where he was working. But, it was not Jon. The caller was Pastor Eric Olsen, the camp director.

Pastor Eric's voice was barely audible as he told me, "Jon was supposed to return to camp last night, but he didn't; and he wasn't at this morning's staff meeting. He's gone missing in the Sawtooth Mountains. The Custer County sheriff has called out a search party..."

As he spoke, my knees went weak; I felt like I might collapse from the weight of this awful message. I had to repeat the terrifying conversation to Linda several times as she tried to absorb the news. Her face tightened in fear; she began to cry. We held onto each other as we fell into a dark world of desperation. Slowly Linda and I began to speak, to think, and to make plans. We were going to Idaho to find our missing son.

The phone rang again. This call came from the sheriff's office in Custer County, Idaho. I felt a surge of hope when a deputy said they found Jon's car. But by the end of the conversation, I understood that it was *just* his car. Jon was still missing.

Before we left for the Minneapolis/St. Paul airport that evening, we called our daughters, Robin, Jocelyn, and Melissa, to tell them their brother was missing, and that we were flying to Idaho to find him. Distraught and crying, the girls each determined to join us there.

Linda and I caught a plane to Denver, and boarded a small propeller aircraft. We landed in Boise late that evening, picked up a rental car, and drove. We spent the rest of the night in a motel in Twin Falls. But we couldn't sleep. Our eyes were swollen from crying.

Early the next morning we drove a narrow, lonely road to Stanley in Central Idaho. The city limits sign read:

Gateway to the Sawtooths
Population 100
Elevation 6,500 feet

A small, rustic town beside the rocky Salmon River, Stanley is surrounded by snowcapped mountains. We counted one grocery store, one gas station, and one motel. The main street was unpaved.

MONDAY, JULY 17, 2006, STANLEY, IDAHO

As prearranged, Linda and I met with two Custer County sheriff's deputies at the Mountain Village Restaurant. Mike was gray-haired and solemn, with a sympathetic expression on his face. Tawny looked too young for a law officer. They briefed us on the "incident," as they called it. Jon's car had been found in the Forest Service Employee section of

THE GRAND MOGUL, SAWTOOTH MOUNTAIN RANGE, CENTRAL IDAHO

the Redfish Lake Lodge. I was too tired and confused to understand the places Mike described. I had never seen the Sawtooth Mountains, Central Idaho, Redfish Lake, or the Salmon River until I went there to search for our missing son.

After meeting with the deputies, we drove out to Sandy Beach on the west side of Redfish Lake. I immediately recognized the configuration of a command center. The parking lot was full of police vehicles and trucks and a large white trailer—the command post. Several people in uniform, sheriffs and forest service employees, were standing in small groups in the hot sun. In the middle, four men were studying a map placed on the hood of a truck. I heard voices over a radio—lots of "radio traffic," as we called it in the Navy.

We were introduced to the Custer County sheriff, Tim Eikens. The sheriff was large and aloof. He walked and talked tall in his pressed uniform. He gave us a perfunctory greeting and turned away. His lack of reassuring words added to our sense of desperation.

For the first time, we met Pastor Eric Olsen and his brother Paul, and Gary Gadwa, a deputy sheriff acting as incident commander (IC). Gary was bearded and woodsy—a diminutive lumberjack. Pastor Eric looked near tears, and collapse. He and Paul were pale and subdued. Eric had reported Jon missing to the sheriff's office at 1:10 p.m. the day before. The search and rescue party had assembled that same afternoon. Today was the first full day of the search.

On this weekday in July, the nearby beach was alive with children and their parents launching boats, swimming, and playing. The picnic area was full of happy vacationers who occasionally glanced at the police activities going on around them.

Linda and I were weary and confused. In a fog of sorrow, we took refuge from the heat in the shade provided by a cluster of pine trees. "This can't be happening," I said. "Jon was a fit and experienced climber—capable, and strong."

I looked up at the mountain to the north, across the lake, the Grand Mogul, the mountain we were told that Jon climbed two days earlier. I prayed to God and to the mountain for Jon's safe return. Each time my prayer ended with, "Jon, I love you." It turned out that I was looking to Mount Heyburn, not the Grand Mogul. After I recognized my mistake, I left Linda resting in the shade and walked alone along the lake and sat down on a rock facing the Grand Mogul. I cried, and prayed some more. The wilderness view and aroma reminded me of Northern Minnesota—a peaceful, clear lake with a rock-covered beach surrounded by fragrant pines trees.

By midafternoon I could hold a thought for more than a few seconds. I slowly began to focus more clearly on the search activity. I overheard the incident commander ask for status reports, repeating again and again on his radio, "Stay on safe and prescribed routes." I walked

over to the group standing over a map on the hood of a truck and introduced myself to Erik Leidecker, a member of the Sawtooth Mountain
Guides, and Greg Dusic from the Forest Service.

Their map was labeled: "The Sawtooth National Recreation Area."
So *that's* where we were. Erik described the terrain on the Grand Mogul
and the locations they were searching. I understood very little of the
conversation, but thanked them, and went back to my refuge in the
shade with Linda.

Our middle daughter, Jocelyn; her husband Doug; and their two
children, three-year-old Audrey and one-year-old Charlie, had arrived
by car from California. They all looked tired. I fell into a long hug
and cry with Jocelyn. She and Doug then sprang into action, meeting
people, and asking questions.

Someone had found the Tom Lopez book, *Idaho: A Climbing Guide*,
on Jon's desk at Luther Heights Camp. Jon's bookmark was a list of
each of the summits he had climbed in the Sawtooth and White Cloud
Mountain Ranges. He had marked page 176, "The Grand Mogul/
Mount Cramer Divide." I devoured the words eagerly for further clues.
Lopez described the area:

> The Sawtooth Range is located completely within the Sawtooth
> National Recreation Area (SNRA), just southwest of Stanley...The
> home of Idaho mountaineering...The range is an extremely rugged
> collection of granite peaks and alpine lakes...Scattered throughout
> the range are 33 peaks that exceed 10,000 feet, and many spires
> and towers crowd the high Sawtooth ridges...The main Sawtooth
> crest stretches for more than 32 miles from north to south. From
> east to west, the range measures 20 miles across at its widest
> point and includes several impressive divides. Thompson peak is
> the highest Sawtooth summit at 10,751 feet...

Although good climbing rock is found throughout the range, the best rock is found in a triangular-shaped area bounded by Red-fish Lake in the north, Hell Roaring Lake in the south and Grand-jean in the west... In addition, Sawtooth Mountain Guides, Idaho's only full-time mountaineering guide service, uses a group of solid granite slabs known as the Super Slabs in Redfish Lake Creek Canyon throughout the summer to teach introductory climbing classes... the Grand Mogul, 9,733 feet. This enticing peak is located at the southwest end of Redfish Lake, where it and Mount Heyburn form ramparts on either side of Redfish Lake Creek. The peak is composed of sections of both hard and deteriorated granite that has formed alternating walls and talus slopes. Little technical climbing has taken place on its slopes.

After reading the Lopez pages, I approached the IC and asked for a briefing. He described the routes of the dog teams and search teams. He said that if Jon had followed the recommended Lopez route, he would have "ascended the avalanche field to the northeast ridge." Lopez did not recommend a descent route off the Grand Mogul.

"Has anyone been to the summit yet?" I asked.

"No," Gary answered.

"Do we know if Jon made it to the summit?" I asked.

"No, we don't," Gary responded.

I asked him to send someone to the summit. He turned to the large group of people standing around and asked for some volunteers. Erik Leidecker and Greg Dusic immediately came forward. They were eager to get onto that mountain.

The team set off, rode the sheriff's boat across Redfish Lake to the trailhead, climbed the Lopez route, and gained the top of the Grand Mogul in less than three hours. On the summit, Erik discovered a summit registry in an old rusty ammunition box where climbers who reach

07/15/06 –
Jon Francis
* LHBC and Ogden, Utah
Climbed avalanche field to
east face and east ridge.
Great times bouldering!
All Glory to God for the
climb and the beautiful Sawtooths.

the peak can sign in. In the box was a card written by Jon. Erik reported that information back to the IC. They discussed which descent route to take, and Erik and Greg chose the southern one called Outside Chance. They returned to the Sandy Beach Staging Area just before sunset. Erik gave Jon's summit registry card to Linda. The three-by-five card had a note handwritten by our son.

In tears, Linda clung tightly to the note and read it over and over again.

After sunset and the evening search team briefing, the incident commander came to me and said, "David, you need to be thinking about giving your son up to the mountain."

I felt a surge of anger. "No! You will not stop searching for Jon after only one day. You need to *find* him!"

Gary went back to the sheriff, then returned and said, "We'll search again tomorrow."

For the next hour, I drifted lamely around, meeting and thanking the many searchers, and petting the search dogs.

As we slowly drove away from that mountain and the vacated search camp, Linda and I felt crushed by sadness and desperation. Someone had booked a room for us at the Mountain Village Lodge in Stanley. For a second night, Linda and I held each other and cried.

Chapter 2

ABANDONED

Like the day before, Tuesday morning was hot in Central Idaho with a predicted high in the mid-nineties. Linda and I ate breakfast mostly in silence at the Mountain Village Restaurant, each in our own dark place. Our server, the mayor of Stanley, introduced herself and expressed her sympathy. I thanked her and she smiled when I commented to her that I guessed she wasn't able to live on her mayor's pay. We left and drove to Sandy Beach for the second day of the search.

Melissa's husband, our newest son-in-law, Steve—a tall, fit, alpine skier—had arrived from Minnesota. A member of the official search team recommended that I charter a plane and fly over the mountain. Steve found a plane and a pilot from Challis Aviation to take us up. While we prepared to fly over the Grand Mogul, the Custer County sheriff showed up and handed me the official candidate registration form for the Minnesota State Senate.

My campaign manager had become aware that I had failed to register, and she had jumped through hoops to get the form to me in Idaho with detailed instructions on how to file. By now, I'd been campaigning for the State Senate for fifteen months and had earned the endorsement of the Minnesota Democratic Farmer Labor (DFL) party that spring.

I nearly tore up the form and threw it away. How could I finish a political campaign under these circumstances? But my sons-in-law, Doug and Steve, advised me to register. "Don't make an important decision like this in your state of mind," Doug cautioned. I put the registration form in my car.

Steve, Doug, and I climbed into the Cessna with Dave, our pilot. We taxied down the grass runway and took off. In less than ten minutes, we were over the Grand Mogul. The mountain loomed huge and ominous. We circled the granite mass repeatedly, trying to focus on the rock surfaces. Bouncing in the updrafts made Doug and me airsick. I watched in amazement as Dave flew the plane, searched the mountain, and handed us airsickness bags.

After an hour in the air, we returned to Stanley's landing strip and lay down on the ground to recover. I reluctantly filled out the campaign registration form and faxed a notarized copy from the Challis Aviation office to the Minnesota Secretary of State.

When we returned to Sandy Beach on Redfish Lake early in the afternoon, the search leaders were wrapping up the day's activities. I regretted taking that flight. It made us sick, wasted time and money, and took me away from the ground search. I was in disbelief, feeling stupid and angry.

Although I knew little about mountain search and rescue, I knew from my submarine "hide and seek" training that you always restart the search at the target's last known position (LKP). Jon's LKP was the summit. Tuesday's search should have focused on determining which descent route Jon took from the summit. The searchers should have gone up to the summit and back down all the logical descent routes. They clearly weren't directed to do that.

My worst fears turned out to be true. The search leaders had decided that Jon was dead. When they failed to find him after a one-day search, they were now just going through the motions. They had concluded, without any physical evidence, that Jon was no longer alive.

The searchers were not being allowed to go off trail, to leave the "safe and prescribed routes." They hadn't been allowed to search all of the logical descent routes. Clearly the more important objective of the officials was to end the search with no injuries to the volunteers.

We did not know then that county sheriffs are kings in their counties. They're not bound by any state or national standards. They can decide to search or to not search, and for how long. Custer County was not in the business of recovering the bodies of lost climbers. I hadn't seen this coming. I remained silent when for a second time the IC said, "David, it's time to give your son up to the mountain." He looked directly at me. All the officers, standing around with their hands on their gun belts, seemed to be in agreement. I was immobilized by disbelief that they had come to this conclusion so quickly. Stunned, I sat paralyzed by a feeling of helplessness.

At the final meeting of the official search team on that evening, I concealed my anger at the authorities for abandoning the search. I told the volunteers how much my family and I appreciated their dedicated work. We shared a deep disappointment that we hadn't found Jon and brought him down from the mountain. Linda and I thanked each tired, distraught searcher. They looked sad but resolved, and each one assured us they would return to find our son.

Linda and I sat on the dock and spoke with Erik Leidecker's partner from the Sawtooth Mountain Guides. Kirk had been one of the spotters in a search helicopter. He gave us Buddhist prayer flags and expressed his sympathy.

As the searchers hugged us and said their final goodbyes, I fell deeper into the abyss of despair. I knew Jon could still be alive on that mountain! I learned during the search that a lost person, who is not seriously injured and has a source of water, can survive for up to seven days. Only three days had passed since Jon went missing. He could be alive, waiting for us, expecting us to find and save him. We were already receiving phone calls from psychics who left voice messages telling us Jon was still alive.

I savagely yearned to go up on the mountain, cradle our son's body in my arms, and carry him away from this cruel and primitive place. But, I knew nothing about search and rescue and never in my life had I climbed a mountain. Only the sheriff had access to professional search and rescue resources. In my view he squandered his authority and failed in his duty.

The search for Francis ended at 7:50 p.m. St. Paul time, said the chief dispatcher for the Custer County sheriff's office. "The official search will not be resuming," said the dispatcher, who declined to give her name.

—MEGAN BOLDT, ST. PAUL PIONEER PRESS. JULY 19, 2006.

Chapter 3

HELP

The Francis family gathered that night and decided to continue the search for Jon despite the fact that no local, state, or federal agencies would help us. Though we knew little about mountain climbing, or search and rescue, we would learn. Hundreds of additional volunteers were streaming into Idaho. We created search teams and missions for dozens of Jon's friends, friends of our family, and people we'd never even met. Jon's running coaches and teammates came. His friends from Lutheran churches, youth groups, and summer camps came. Strangers from Idaho and neighboring states joined us. My friends, our daughters' friends, people from all across the U.S., guests at the Redfish Lake Lodge, and some volunteers from the official search party returned, eager to go back on the mountain. At our request, we received the water-stained map that showed the "safe and prescribed routes" of the unsuccessful, twenty-nine-hour "official" search effort.

I numbered the days:

Day One. Saturday, July 15, 2006: Jon gained the summit of the Grand Mogul.

Day Two. Sunday, July 16: Jon was reported missing and the official search party assembled.

CUSTER COUNTY, IDAHO SEARCH MAP

Day Three. Monday, July 17: the first full day of search.

Day Four. Tuesday, July 18: the second day of searching, and the day public officials and law enforcement abandoned our son.

Day Five. Wednesday, July 19: Sawtooth National Recreation Area (SNRA), Idaho

We set up our makeshift command and control headquarters in the outdoor picnic area of the Redfish Lake Lodge. The owners of the lodge, Jeff and Audra, were gracious and supportive. Their rustic lodge offered shelter, bathroom facilities, food, and beverages. We plugged into the electrical outlet for the bandstand to power our electronics.

Jocelyn's husband Doug was appointed search manager because he had the most mountain climbing experience, having climbed in the Rockies and the Sierras. Our oldest daughter, Robin, arrived from New York and took over media relations, her specialty. Hourly, we were contacted for interviews by newspaper, radio, and television reporters throughout the country. Channel 7, from Boise, parked a satellite TV transmission truck at the swimming beach at Redfish Lake.

Since neither the sheriff's office nor the Forest Service was required or willing to, Jocelyn created a handmade missing-person flier containing Jon's picture. She alternated between angry wails and tears as she nailed pictures of her missing brother at trailheads in the Sawtooths, Stanley outfitters, and on Forest Service bulletin boards.

Linda took charge of the budget and spending necessary to pay for the search. She was our banker, bookkeeper, treasurer, and travel agent. I handled most of the phone communications and logistics. Since our cell phones didn't work, we began calling Stanley "Communications Hell." I struggled to stay on the line with Governor Tim Pawlenty of Minnesota, who called to relay his concern for Jon, and his efforts to get the official Idaho search restarted.

Jo Jo Fuller, on staff at the Redfish Lake Lodge, loaned us her satellite phone. It wasn't perfect, but it worked most of the time and reconnected us to the outside world. Another Redfish Lake Lodge staff

MISSING SINCE JULY 15, 2006
JON FRANCIS

24 Years Old
5' 4" in Height
130 Pounds
Curly Brown Hair
Brown Eyes

Last seen wearing:
Dark hat
Aqua colored shirt
Tie-dyed undershirt
Unknown pants
Approach-type shoes

Carrying a daypack
Probably yellow in color

Last Known Position:	Jon gained the summit of **Grand Mogul** in the late morning of July 15th, 2006 via the Northeast Ridge.
Possible Plans:	Jon may have descended via his ascent route, the East Face, Outside Chance, or attempted to link summits with Elephant's Perch, Braxon Peak, or others.

Please help us find Jon!

If you may have seen Jon or have any information, please contact Jeff Hasse President, Search, Rescue, and Recovery Resources of Minnesota at 612-722-5786.

If you find Jon, please call the CUSTER COUNTY SHERIFF at 208-879-2232.

member introduced herself. Greta had been on the morning shuttle boat ride with Jon on Saturday.

The Redfish Lake Lodge shuttle boats carry campers and climbers on the five-mile trip across Redfish Lake to the Transfer Camp Site. Greta and her father, Tom, had taken family photographs on the boat, and Jon happened to appear in the background. As far as we knew, Tom was the last person to speak with Jon.

Tom recalled seeing Jon leave the shuttle boat and briskly hike the trailhead leading to the Grand Mogul. Greta printed a copy of the photograph for us. On the boat, Jon was wearing his favorite aqua, long-sleeved Coolmax shirt. I noticed the contemplative look on his face. I'd seen that look many times when he prepared for athletic competitions.

Jon ran competitively for ten years and earned All State, All American, and National Championship honors. Before a race, he would go deep, and mentally prepare himself for the run. But this time, he was mentally preparing for a difficult mountain climb.

At family search headquarters, Pastor Dan Rieke, from Our Savior Lutheran Church in Twin Falls, Idaho, became our secretary. In a spiral notebook he recorded information on the volunteers and their search assignments. Pastor Dan met our son when Jon conducted a weeklong Bible Day Camp at his church.

Bart Green, an attorney from Boise, acted as my legal counsel and cool head. The week before climbing the Grand Mogul, Jon stayed with Bart and his family while leading a day camp at their church in Boise, King of Glory Lutheran. A friend of mine from Minnesota donated his corporate jet to fly in several searchers, two trackers, our youngest daughter, Melissa, and our grandchildren, ten-year-old Katie and four-year-old Stephen. My friend, fellow Navy Reserve captain and mentor Dave Recker, was also on that flight. His energy and enthusiasm immediately raised my spirits.

We were overwhelmed with media interest and calls asking for information or offering help. I spent sixteen hours a day returning phone calls and screening and thanking volunteers while trying to stay on top of the search tactics and clues.

Many times I stood in silent admiration, watching our daughter Robin work. Confident and businesslike, she maintained grace under pressure. Cool in a crisis, she prepared press releases and handled media interviews and chaos.

Robin issued the first Francis family press release to a list of media contacts she had assembled. The press release reflected our anger and desperation.

24-year-old Hiker Lost:
Idaho Authorities Abandon Search Early
Contact: Robin Francis

Jon Francis, 24, last seen Saturday, Grand Mogul trail, Idaho. Authorities call off search after only 2 days. Son of MN State Senate Democratic Candidate David Francis, and employee of Luther Heights Bible Camp.

24-year-old Jon Francis, of Stillwater, MN, set out Saturday morning on a day hike up the Grand Mogul trail in rugged Sawtooth Mountains, Idaho. He reached the summit but did not return. Francis, an avid outdoorsman and experienced hiker, told friends at the Luther Heights Bible Camp where he worked that he would return by 6 p.m. When he failed to show up, staff alerted authorities.

Sunday, the Custer County Sheriff's office launched a search party but abandoned efforts Tuesday night after only 2 days, leaving Francis' family and friends to continue the search alone. Jon is the son of David Francis, a Democratic candidate for Minnesota State Senate, who immediately flew to Idaho with friends and family to lead an independent search for Jon. Jon is described as deeply religious and mature. Distraught friends and family are pouring into Idaho to continue the daylight search, but more manpower and official support is needed.

Tourism to Idaho State Parks is the state's third-leading industry hosting over 2 million visitors a year; but are tourists and outdoor enthusiasts really safe? Authorities provided a conservative search but simply gave up when initial efforts failed to locate Francis. Idaho authorities only explored the summit, where Francis was last seen, after urging from David Francis.

The Francis family and friends believe Jon is alive and in need of immediate assistance; Minnesota residents are outraged and engaged. Minnesota congressmen and senators are talking with counterparts in Idaho; Episcopal and Lutheran bishops are working with Idaho delegations and contacting the governor as friends and family come to Idaho to launch a search for Francis.

The Francis family urges State officials to re-engage their search, and they call for the help of experienced hikers and guides to locate their missing son.

FIND JON: Keep Idaho Looking

Time was now our worst enemy. Friday, July 21, would be Day Seven. If Jon was still alive, we needed to find him before Saturday. We felt uplifted when our first volunteer dog handler and search dog arrived. It was Jim Hanley and his dog Shania, a border collie from South Dakota. Jim, wearing an Australian slouch hat, looked like he had arrived from the outback. He was immediately surrounded by a crowd of volunteers who warmly welcomed him.

I approached Jim to ask about Shania's capabilities. We soon discovered we were fraternity brothers. He was a former Navy corpsman, so he immediately assumed the role of first-aid person and treated the cut I'd just gotten on my leg. He could see that I was under emotional distress but working hard to organize the operation. I was at battle stations with an intense focus on the activity and problem solving. But, I had no checklist to follow that would help me find my lost son. Jim walked over to meet Linda, who was sitting alone on the beach, staring at the mountain.

Linda said, "Thank God. A dog who will find our son." Linda and I hoped that this search dog would lead us to Jon's chosen descent route. Unfortunately, Shania's early efforts yielded no clues.

Dozens of friends and volunteers arrived with provisions and equipment including much-needed two-way radios. Many sat quietly with us in prayer. Tom and Nancy Austin, from our church in Stillwater, arrived. She cooked while he climbed.

Within a few days, we managed to organize and send 120 "heartbeats" (a person or a dog) onto the Grand Mogul and bring them all back safely. Several heartbeats searched multiple times. We suffered only one minor injury that week. Doug's friend John from Washington State fell and cut his nose, requiring six stitches.

Meanwhile, the television reporter from Channel 7 in Boise told me that the Republican acting governor of Idaho, Lieutenant Governor James Risch, was coming to Redfish Lake to meet with us. I was annoyed at the news—we needed search dogs, not politicians. Although I was concerned about this distraction from our efforts, I felt a faint hope that the governor might bring more resources to help us find Jon.

Chapter 4

POLITICAL AIR COVER

Day Six. Thursday, July 20, 2006, SNRA, Idaho

At the end of Day Six, when all of our searchers were safely off the mountain, Linda, Robin, and I sat on the Redfish Lake dock waiting for the governor of Idaho. We had not been given a time or a meeting place.

Jim Risch had been lieutenant governor of Idaho until May 2006 when he replaced Governor Dirk Kempthorne, who was now President George W. Bush's Secretary of the Interior. The sun was setting when a sheriff's deputy arrived to inform us that Governor Risch was waiting for us at the Redfish Lake Visitor's Center. We had no idea where that was, so we followed the deputy in our car.

Once in the Visitor's Center conference room we found ourselves vastly outnumbered by state officials and law enforcement officers in uniform. Mrs. Risch, fashionably dressed, was the one friendly face in the room. She greeted us warmly and expressed her condolences. Governor Risch sat at the head of the table. Dressed in coat and tie, he was a slim, balding man, about my height and age. He rose to shake my hand.

I immediately felt ill prepared for the meeting. I had spent the entire day immersed in a desperate search for my son; I was hardly ready for a business meeting with the governor of Idaho. In my thirty years of military, public, and business experience, I planned and led many important meetings. I had told truth to power and faced tough negotiators. But that evening, I was a grieving father—groping in a fog of sorrow.

Quickly, we were broadsided with a scripted message. The governor basically said that the Francis family was risking the lives of others by continuing our search without professional resources. I responded by stating the obvious: that we were desperately *trying* to get professional SAR personnel—especially search dogs—but they would not come to our aid without the sheriff's authorization, and that the Custer County sheriff would not provide authorization. I added that our efforts were being hampered by State-sponsored radio announcements telling people not to come to Idaho to search for Jon Francis. At one point in the meeting, Robin saw Sheriff Eikens and Gary Gadwa roll their eyes.

The governor repeated the scripted message—that the official search was over, and if we continued to put people on the mountain, the Francis family would be responsible for any injuries or deaths. At the end of the monologues, we were asked to step outside while the officials reached a decision concerning any further State action.

When we were ushered back into the conference room, the governor said that Idaho would provide us with search aircraft and a National Guard communications truck over the weekend. I thanked the governor and we left.

Immediately after the meeting, I regretted not giving voice to my family's pain. I wish I had been able to say:

"Governor, if that were your son on the Grand Mogul, would you be satisfied with a three-day search resulting in no recovery?"

And, "Governor, you wouldn't have had to travel all this way if the sheriff had done his job."

Or, "Sheriff, you are an elected official responsible for search and rescue in a county that is eighty percent wilderness. Your lack of resources, preparation, effort, and commitment border on negligence and dereliction of duty."

Day Seven. Friday, July 21, 2006, SNRA, Idaho

To prevent interference between ground searchers and aircraft, we were ordered off the mountain. I believed that this was the last day our son could still be alive. The governor had deployed helicopters with infrared, and search aircraft with some kind of spectral imaging technology. We sat in frustration as a helicopter with heat-seeking capabilities flew over the sun-baked mountain during the hottest part of the day.

We were given no information from state or local authorities. Everything we learned came from the media. We wanted to place feet, eyes, and noses on the mountain that day, not questionable technology. The aircraft found nothing. We did not know then that in a wilderness search for a non-responsive, missing person, helicopters and search aircraft are the least effective.

We documented the pointless activities that prevented us from searching on the mountain:

Daily Search Summary
Jonathan David Francis
Friday, July 21, 2006

Resources Involved:
Custer County Search and Rescue (unconfirmed)
Sawtooth Search and Rescue
Gary Gadwa, IC (principally coordinating flights)

U.S. Forest Service personnel
Air National Guard
Civil Air Patrol
Sawtooth Mountain Guides (SMG)
Family and friends of subject

Summary of Missions:
Helicopter Team (Air National Guard UH1-N helicopter)
Personnel: pilot, crew chief, Ryan Jung (SMG), 2-3 others
Mission: Air search using forward-looking infrared radar (FLIR) and
    observers. 50-100 feet off deck.
Results: FLIR was used for approximately 20 minutes then discon-
    tinued due to ineffectiveness under current conditions.
Approximately 5-hour flight time between two flights.
No clues found.

Ryan Jung, one of the Sawtooth Mountain Guides, rode in the helicopter and described his frustration regarding the five-and-a-half-hour
search. In an interview afterward with Dana Dugan of the *Idaho Mountain Express* he said, "The crew engineer operated the forward-looking
infrared system, known as FLIR. The screen is only 7 to 8 inches. It's
good for surveillance or to stop intruders, but it doesn't work for looking in three-dimensional topography. The human eye is more sensitive
to color. I asked if a body would show, and the crew said it wouldn't."

I had to hand it to this new governor. He was clearly a skillful
politician and artful dodger. In the public eye, he responded to political
pressure, came to the rescue of local law enforcement, and appeared to
be providing help in our time of need. But we needed people and dogs.
What we got was political air cover for Idaho's elected officials.

DAY EIGHT. SATURDAY, JULY 22, 2006, SNRA, IDAHO

Jon was most likely no longer alive. But I was too numb to mourn the death of our only son. When the Idaho National Guard communications truck arrived, I stepped inside to use the high-tech communications devices to maintain contact with the search parties and return dozens of phone messages.

But the sergeant said, "No. I'm sorry, you can't stay in here. You are not authorized. We will put a telephone outside for you." So I took my position at a card table with the telephone.

Day Eight looked like a law enforcement convention. The Francis family volunteers were allowed back on the mountain while dozens of official observers stood watch. The superintendent of the Minnesota Bureau of Criminal Apprehension (BCA) had flown out two BCA agents to be with us. Several county sheriffs and deputies stood around with their hands on their gun belts. Although it appeared as if we had more observers than searchers, we put more volunteers on the mountain Saturday and Sunday, who searched the summit, the east side, the west side, portions of the south, and parts of the north face. It was a wide search, but we failed to find any trace of Jon. Our search manager, son-in-law Doug, completed our first search map using his daughter Audrey's crayons, showing in color codes the areas on the Grand Mogul that we had covered. The crayon-annotated map, along with the handwritten diary kept by Pastor Dan, documented our family-led search effort.

At the same time, I needed to deal with the politics swirling around my head. I became concerned that our public expressions of anger at Idaho officials might be misinterpreted as a lack of appreciation for the outpouring of support from countless Idaho volunteers.

Robin wrote a second press release. This one expressed our sincere gratitude.

25

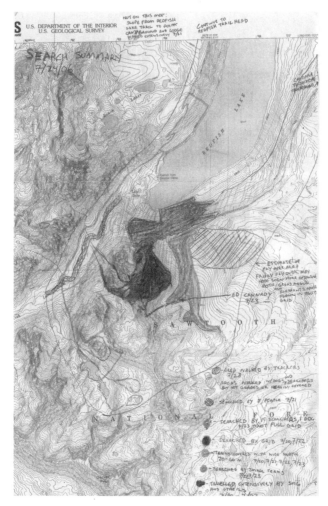

COLOR-CODED SEARCH SUMMARY BY DOUG PLASS, USING
AUDREY'S CRAYONS

We must have put hundreds of dollars worth of calls on Jo Jo Fuller's satellite phone. We asked her to send us the bill.

"No," she said. It was her "gift" to us. Hers was one of countless acts of selflessness and generosity that came from the people of Idaho and from people across the country.

Chapter 5

VIGILS

By late Sunday afternoon, July 23, eight days after Jon went missing, we were mentally and physically exhausted. I ached with the knowledge that Jon was gone. Never again could I hold him, hug him, or hear him call me "Dad." I was robbed of his presence and his future.

Sunday evening, after all of the searchers were safely off the mountain, Doug came to me in tears, saying, "David, we didn't find Jon. I'm sorry." As I embraced my son-in-law I thanked him for his awesome effort and love.

We gathered in a circle on the Shore of Redfish Lake in view of the Grand Mogul. Pastor Dan led us in prayer. His words were comforting and wrenching. For the first time since Linda and I arrived in Idaho, the sky looked dark, angry, and ominous. As black clouds hovered over the Grand Mogul, I directed my thoughts again and again toward the mountain: *Jon, I love you. Jon, I miss you. I lift you up and place you in the arms of God.*

Finally, I asked in lament, *God, where were you? Why didn't you guide Jon's feet off that mountain?*

Our family said thank you and farewell to the last of the volunteers. We drove, as if in a funeral procession, to Sawtooth City where Jocelyn had rented a house for the family. We were all together—our three daughters, two sons-in-law, and four grandchildren. But we were not complete. Jon was not there.

Sawtooth City, population fifteen, is situated near Smiley Creek, about twenty miles south of Stanley. We now had access to an actual landline telephone; I sat at the kitchen table and returned dozens of voicemails. I returned several calls from the Episcopal Bishop of Minnesota. Bishop Jelinek knew Jon from his involvement with the Diocesan Youth Group. They had traveled to Washington D.C. together on a pilgrimage to the National Cathedral. He had written letters and made phone calls to the governor, senators, and representatives of Idaho, encouraging the officials to renew the search for Jon.

RE: DISAPPEARANCE OF JON FRANCIS IN SAWTOOTH MOUNTAINS, IDAHO

Jon Francis has been lost in the woods of the Sawtooth Mountains for six days. He is a fine young man whom I have known for years. Both he and his family have been faithful members of Ascension Episcopal Church in Stillwater. Jon is exceptionally dedicated to both youth and the environment as an expression of his faith.

As many are aware from media coverage, Jon went missing on Saturday, July 15, 2006. I am very distressed that rescue efforts were called off Tuesday, July 18, 2006. I have contacted Governor Jim Risch of Idaho, as have numerous of our Minnesota representatives and senators, both statewide and national.

If anyone who reads or hears this has any influence in the state of Idaho in trying to persuade officials to continue this search, now is the time to act. For the rest of us who do not have such influence, now is the time to pray.

The Rt. Rev. James L. Jelinek
VIII Bishop
Episcopal Diocese of Minnesota

I returned phone messages from members of the Minnesota State Legislature: Senate Majority Leader Dean Johnson (also a Lutheran pastor and a brigadier general, Chaplain Corps, Minnesota National Guard), and State Senators Ann Rest and Becky Lourey (a Gold Star Mother whose son had been killed in Iraq). There were messages from Minnesota Governor Tim Pawlenty; Minnesota's Commissioner of Public Safety, Michael Campion; members of the Minnesota Congressional Delegation who had lobbied their counterparts in Idaho to continue the search; messages of support and sympathy from Episcopal and Lutheran church leaders as well as members; and friends, relatives, and countless friends of Jon. We received offers of sympathy and help from many I didn't know.

Patty Wetterling called to express her sympathy and to extend an offer of help from the Jacob Wetterling Foundation (JWF). She and her husband, Jerry, had established JWF in February 1990, four months after their eleven-year-old son Jacob was abducted at gunpoint by a masked man near his home in St. Joseph, Minnesota. Since then, JWF has worked to find missing children and to educate children, teens, parents, caregivers, and teachers about personal safety.

I called Father Jerry Doherty, our priest at Ascension Episcopal Church in Stillwater. Jerry was not just my priest; he was also one of my closest friends and confidants. The Francis and Doherty families had camped together in the Boundary Waters Canoe Area Wilderness in Northern Minnesota. Jerry and others led a candlelight vigil at Ascension church in Stillwater, shortly after Jon went missing.

Jerry had known Jon since he was nine, and Jon had worked for Jerry one summer. Jerry, who loved Jon like a son, flew to Idaho to be with us. We met the next day at Luther Heights Bible Camp. I felt immediately comforted by his presence.

That day was another in what seemed to be an endless series of beautiful days—almost a perfect day. The sun was bright in a cloudless, crystal-blue sky. The air was warm; the winds were light. We were surrounded by beauty—snow-capped mountains, lush pine trees, and a shimmering lake. But I hated all of the perfection. This was the lake that carried Jon to the mountain. The tall trees watched silently as he climbed. "All Glory to God for the beautiful Sawtooths," Jon had written on the mountain that I now regarded as soulless and savage.

Father Jerry was able to express the anger, confusion, and sense of outrage that afflicted all of us. He had lived and ministered in Montana for many years and understood the Western culture that seemed willing to bow to the mystique and power of the mountain—and believe that it was a beautiful place to die. I didn't share that sentiment. Jerry and I agreed that abandoning a loved one on a mountain was insane.

I had to hold my anger in check whenever someone said to me, "Jon is in a beautiful place. It is where he wanted to be."

A few times I found the courage to reply, "No. Jon wanted to come down from the mountain and go back to camp to do the work he enjoyed with the youth he loved."

I was never able to say aloud the truth that lived in the darkest corner of my mind: "This mountain is *not* a beautiful place. My son's body is now at the bottom of the food chain where it will be destroyed by the elements and devoured by predators!"

Father Jerry and my family took the shuttle boat on a pilgrimage to the foot of the Grand Mogul. In sight of the mountain's north face, Jerry read from Psalm 121.

Together we cried, prayed, and stared mindlessly at the mountain. One by one, we talked about Jon, how much we loved him, and what a difference he made in our lives. Melissa added that she couldn't remember a time when her brother complained about another person.

He met people where they were and loved them as they were. I saw that in Jon, too.

The grandchildren wanted to go swimming, so Melissa rose and took them into the cold water of the lake. As I watched my young grandchildren playing in the water, I saw life. But when I looked up, I saw only death, the stark mountain of loss.

A Song of Ascents
Psalm 121 (NRSV)

I lift my eyes to the hills
from where will my help come?
My help comes from the Lord,
who made heaven and earth.

He will not let your foot be moved;
he who keeps you will not slumber.
He who keeps Israel
will neither slumber nor sleep.

The Lord is your keeper;
the Lord is your shade at your right hand.
The sun shall not strike you by day,
nor the moon by night.
The Lord will keep you from all evil;
he will keep your life.
The Lord will keep your going out and your coming in
from this time on and forevermore.

SUNDAY, JULY 30, LUTHER HEIGHTS BIBLE CAMP

Our next vigil was at Luther Heights Bible Camp where Jon spent four wonderful summers as a counselor. We met his friends, his mentors, and staff; all were in shock and mourning. We found Cara, Jon's friend and frequent climbing partner, alone and crying under a cluster of trees. Linda and I went with the camp leaders and staff again across Redfish Lake to the Transfer Camp and sat in a circle around a campfire pit. I thought back to the many campfires over the years when I sat with Jon and our extended family, telling stories, staring into the fire, feeling close and content.

Here there was no campfire, but Jon's friends told stories about him. We listened to examples of how Jon brought love, joy, and fun to all his relationships. His mentor, Laura, shared that Jon told her he'd finally made a decision to attend seminary to become a pastor. I'd known that Jon was struggling with a sense of call to ordained ministry. I felt pride at the news, and pain that he would not complete that goal.

At this campfire circle I began to see Jon not as my little boy but as a man, a remarkable young man, who loved deeply and was deeply loved. *How did I miss this?*

We left the fire circle vigil and returned to Sawtooth City. To continue our search we needed to make tough decisions. First we decided to engage Erik Leidecker and the Sawtooth Mountain Guides (SMG) to help and advise us on continuing search efforts. They knew the Sawtooths better than anyone.

Erik was intelligent and fit. He was a Dartmouth graduate, a literature major who combined his passion—back country activities—with his occupation. Erik and his partner Kirk led whitewater rafting trips, mountain climbing, backpacking, and wilderness hiking and camping groups. He enjoyed extreme sports like winter skiing on the Sawtooth slopes. Although he was compassionate, he was also realistic about SMG's limited ability to find Jon.

During the week of July 27 the Sawtooth Mountain Guides spent several days climbing and searching. They reported a foul smell (detectable by the human nose) and attempted to locate it. I tried to push out of my mind the horrible image this created.

Jon's body was now decomposing. Our son's remains were attracting scavengers. We needed to find him before his body was stolen from us.

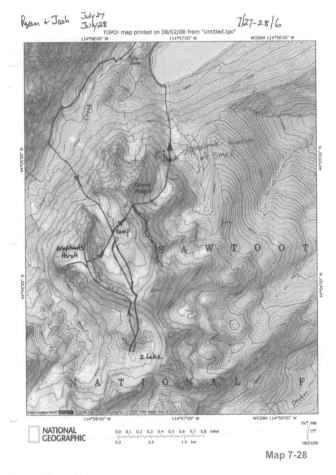

Map 7-28

Map of Foul Odor

33

Chapter 6

PREDATOR

I find it incredible that anyone would take advantage of grieving parents and defraud them of money. But it happened to us only two weeks after Jon went missing. Volunteers were no longer coming to Idaho, and we were groveling for search dog resources. In our desperation, we engaged a dog handler from the West Coast. A friend of mine met him on an airplane and sent us his card. I spoke with Frank* over the phone, and he assured me that his dog, Jesse*, would find Jon.

Frank offered us a special rate of $1,700 for his services. When I met him in Stanley, I instantly felt uneasy. He came across like a carnival hustler. I should have given him gas money and sent him home. Frank, his dog Jesse, our mountain guide Erik, and a capable and dedicated volunteer from Boise, Idaho, called Sean Duffy started their climb on the Grand Mogul at six p.m. on Saturday, July 29, and set up an overnight camp.

The next morning, Linda and I were full of hope as we drove to the Redfish Lake Lodge to meet with Frank and Erik for breakfast. Frank described Jesse's series of "death alerts" and his firm conclusion that Jon was dead, and that his body was located to the south of the mountain.

The absurdity of paying a person seventeen hundred dollars to tell us that our son was dead somewhere on the mountain did not register

*Not their real names.

at first. Linda numbly wrote out a check to Frank for seventeen hundred dollars.

That evening I received a call from a reporter at *NewWest.Net* asking me to confirm a story that Jon's remains had been found by a search dog named Jesse. "No. Jon has not been found. It's not true," I told her. This set off an alarm. I immediately concluded that Frank had reported the bogus story. We stopped payment on his check, and sent him an email accusing him of fraud. He denied any involvement and threatened to sue. The reporter confirmed that Frank was not the source of the story and I sent a letter of apology to him with a check for $1,200.

Dear Frank:

Again, let me apologize for the check stoppage. You were not responsible for the painful press release that went to news wire. In the meantime, we have had a chance to assess your value in the search and your performance.

You over-promised and underperformed. In retrospect, you did not cover the amount of area on the mountain we expected. We contacted you to find our son, Jon. You did not. Your dog may be capable of divining whether Jon is dead or alive, but you were not capable of following Jesse to where our son is resting. That was our expectation.

We have had many search and rescue teams come in to help. All of them charged us for travel and lodging, only. You are the only one to bill us for an hourly rate.

Enclosed is a check for $1,200. This covers $500 for travel and lodging ($25/hour), $200 for gas and $500 for a daily fee for you and your dog.

I expect that this payment will close the books on our business relationship. Taking legal action against us would cause irreparable damage to your reputation. We feel strongly that you took advantage of parents in grief. I encourage you to let this matter go.

Sincerely,

David Francis

We did not hear from Frank again. When we reviewed the written search report he submitted, we reconstructed his route. He hadn't even known where he was. He was on the northeast side of the mountain, not the northwest side as he'd recorded.

Frank's Search Report [errors included]

07-29-06 1800Hrs. Eric, myself, along with my search dog and another support climber named Shawn, started up the northwestern trail headed towards the nw corner of Grand Mogol. As we conducted a night search operation SAR Dog Jesse alerted to Jon's scent, giving an immediate "Death Alert" in the water at the base of the trail in Red Fish Lake. There were several run off streams feeding into this water source. We made our way up to through the treeline.

The winds were consistent at 10-20 mph gusts directly from the south. Search dog Jesse consistently gave major death alerts from (air scent alerts) into the winds from the south. We searched up to the 8000 ft level and SAR Dog Jesse consistently alerted to the south. We concluded our night search efforts at 0800 on 07-30-06. Took a boat the North shore of Red Fish Lake and debriefed Mr. and Mrs. Francis.

With the winds coming directly from the south through out the search mý findings are as follows. I feel that there is a 90% probability of POA, probability of area, based on the wind direction and my dogs constant death alerts that Jon is on the South side of the search area.

I find in 100% of my cases over the last 34 years, that if the victim is decease, He or she will come to a family member in a dream and tell or show them what happened to them and where they are (area wise). When I debrief the family members and if we do find the victim, their dreams are 100% accurate on our findings.

Chapter 7

PSYCHICS, SEARCHERS, AND SHERIFFS

Tuesday, August 1, 2006, Linda's birthday, Stanley, Idaho

We originally planned to be in Idaho with Jon for Linda's birthday, before he moved back to Utah. In our rustic surroundings, there was no Hallmark store. I felt fortunate to find a birthday card for her at Stanley's Gift and Fishing Tackle. We had moved into a trailer in Stanley, generously provided by lodge owners Jeff and Audra.

Despite the refusal of law enforcement to authorize further resources, several sympathetic individuals and groups ignored personal risk and politics to come to our aid. Among them were Paula McCollum and Jeb, a North Carolina hound dog, and Susan Janz and canine Susie, both from Treasure Valley Search Dogs in Boise. Paula, an outstanding dog handler and search resource, ran a search dog training school. She and Susan were members of the official search team in July, and they returned on August 1 with their dogs.

Jeff Hasse and Ken Anderson, the founders of Search, Rescue, and Recovery Resources of Minnesota, arrived. Nancy Sabin, executive director of the Jacob Wetterling Foundation, had sent them. Jeff and Ken were bearded, sleepy, and disheveled in appearance, but the work they did was meticulous. In the back room of the Sawtooth Mountain Guides' office in Stanley, they set to work, reconstructing all of the prior search missions. They interviewed us, the Sawtooth Mountain Guides, and the sheriff's department. For days, they labored twenty hours a day, documenting the previous search and creating topographical maps using a computer software program. The maps contained searcher names, search routes, and a scientific assessment of the areas covered. We began applying the concept of POD (probability of detection).

Linda and I were given the assignment of starting a "subject profile" of our son. This required questioning Jon's friends and climbing partners about his abilities, personality, health, fitness, outdoor experience, relationships, concerns, and decision making. How did Jon make decisions on the ascent and on his descent? Was he a risk taker? What other mountains had he climbed? What was his skill level? Jon's profile was an important source of clues to aid and direct our search.

> Jon loved physical challenges. He was somewhat afraid of heights and used climbing to overcome it. He is described as sometimes being too self-sufficient. He didn't ask for help or advice much. He is described as a leader, but knew when to follow.

> —EXCERPT FROM THE REPORT OF
> SEARCH MANAGER JEFF HASSE

At the same time, several "psychics" offered their help. I had no experience with this supernatural dimension and I was skeptical, considering them a distraction. But Linda, Erik, and I discussed the psychic visions and how to deal with this information. We decided to regard whatever psychics provided as possible clues, and pursue them if they made sense. Our first such clue came from a psychic named Colleen, who told us that Jon was still alive. He was injured, especially his right leg. Jill, a psychic from Minnesota, called to say that Jon had found shelter by crawling into an opening in the mountain. We would be able to see his shoes. She drew a map with a view of mountain peaks where Jon was located. We carried the drawing with us. Linda made a transparency from it, and we often held it up to the mountain looking for a matching view. Unfortunately, everywhere we looked in the Sawtooths were nearly identical craggy mountain peaks. Another psychic, Maureen, told us, "Jon went in the wrong direction right away." Glen, a dowser from Idaho, sent us the elevation and UTM (universal transverse Mercator) system coordinates where his professional dowser tool indicated Jon's location. Erik and his guides added these "clues" to his list of areas to be searched.

Family of missing hiker not giving up: Jon Francis missing 19 days now

—Dana Dugan, *Idaho Mountain Express,* August 3, 2006

"The search continues," David Francis said. A retired Navy captain and nuclear submarine officer, Francis, who is in the middle of a campaign for the Minnesota State Senate, sat on a shady porch with his wife Linda and discussed the search for his son. His Naval training was coming in handy. He held himself together almost until the end of the conversation. His wife kept very still and quiet.

Jon Francis, 24, was spending his fourth summer at the Luther Bible Camp near Alturas Lake, north of Ketchum, when he disappeared Saturday, July 15, while climbing the 9,733-foot Grand Mogul in the Sawtooth Mountains. He had been working as the director of youth ministry at Ascension Lutheran Church in Ogden, Utah…

I was annoyed that the newspaper articles kept referring to Jon as a hiker. He was more than a hiker; Jon was a skilled mountain climber. There is no trail to the summit of the Grand Mogul. Reaching the summit required scrambling through scree (gravel-like, slippery, decaying granite), and climbing over and around huge boulders.

On August 4, two dog teams, High Country Search Dogs and Wyoming K9 SAR, arrived from the Jackson Hole area in Wyoming. The highly capable teams were led by Janet Wilts, a gently gruff, no-nonsense woman. The team's energy, professionalism, skills, and confidence raised our hopes. They thoroughly covered the eastern side, surrounding forest, and drainage areas.

Chuck Schneebeck, a lean, athletic man in his late sixties, climbed to the summit of the Grand Mogul with his dog, Buster. This was the first time any of the search dogs made it to the summit. Buster was carried in a sling part of the way. This extraordinary search effort provided several dog scent indications (clues of Jon's presence); but Jon was not found.

Once again, numb and despondent, I shared a meal and spoke with the tired and saddened team. I thanked them for their dedicated efforts and deep caring. I was losing hope that we would ever find Jon and lay him to rest.

By August 7, all of the volunteers left Idaho, and we had no other search teams committed. Linda and I decided it was time to gather Jon's belongings and return to Minnesota.

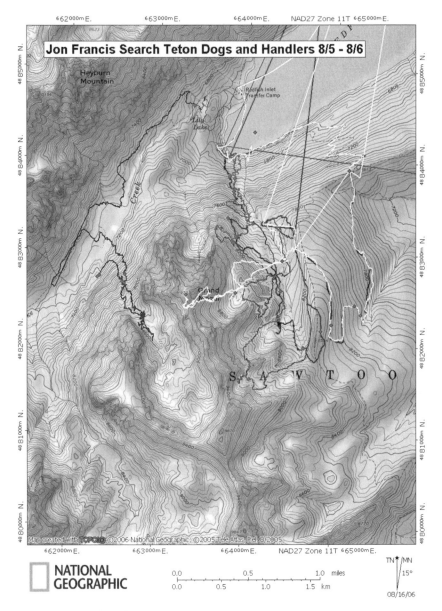

GRAND TETON TEAM SEARCH

Chapter 8

JONATHAN DAVID FRANCIS

Jonathan David Francis. We had his name picked out for twenty-two years. Linda and I were high school sweethearts. On a trip to Northern Michigan in 1960, we talked about a time when we would be married, have children together, and raise a family. We agreed to name our first-born son Jonathan David. Jonathan is Hebrew for "God's gift" or "gift of God," and David means "beloved."

Linda went into labor in the late evening so we checked into the Northfield hospital. This was our fourth birth. We didn't know whether this child was male or female. Linda's labor progressed quickly, and by two a.m. our doctor appeared. He reminded me of Marcus Welby, the reassuring television doctor. The baby was in a hurry to arrive.

Too late for pain medicine, Linda gave birth the natural way in the early morning. I was with her, and so proud of her strength. She was not a screamer. She uttered low moans, and breathed rapidly in and out. Soon I saw the dark-haired head appear — then a face with familiar Francis features — and finally, a small body. I spotted the male genitals just as Dr. Halvorson announced, "It's a boy!"

Jonathan David Francis was born! Someone I had waited for my entire life finally arrived. The doctor placed our son into Linda's arms.

DAVID WITH TWO-DAY-OLD JONATHAN

He had my dark-brown hair, a handsome face, and sincere brown eyes that I thought reflected his Irish heritage. Our son was small, as all of our babies were — less than six pounds. Although Jonathan spent his first day in an incubator, he was healthy. I believe that God danced the day Jonathan was born.

The morning low was 11 degrees and the afternoon high was 24 on Jon's first day. But there was a hope of spring. The birth of our son and the prospect of spring warmth gave me an indescribable sense of joy and optimism. I thought of Jonathan in the cycle of life as natural heir to the love and closeness of my wise and compassionate grandmother, Myrtle Francis, who had recently passed away at ninety-two.

Our daughters, neighbors, and friends were excited when we brought Jonathan home. Jonathan made my life complete. He made me feel whole. Our family was now fully formed. We had three beautiful daughters, ages eleven, fourteen, and sixteen, and the son Linda and I had held in our hearts for twenty-two years. From the beginning, Jon's sisters surrounded him with love and attention. They cuddled with him, watched over him, dressed and fed him.

> "And it came to pass...that the soul of Jonathan was knit with the soul of David and Jonathan loved him as his own soul."
> 1 Samuel, 18 (NRSV)

When our daughters were babies, I was in the U.S. Navy, going to sea as a submarine sailor and later as an officer. While I was on active duty, Linda and I had three children in five years, but I was seldom home to help with our girls. I missed so much of the joy *and* the hard work of their early months.

Jonathan was my first chance to be present during the baby months. I cherished that time—the baths, the nighttime feedings, even the diaper changes. I rocked Jonathan and fed him his supplemental bottle, relishing our time together in the quiet beauty of the night.

Because Easter arrived shortly after Jonathan's birth, we prepared for his baptism, and the confirmation of fourteen-year-old Jocelyn, at the Great Vigil of Easter on April 10, 1982. Their combined spiritual rituals was a portend of the close relationship that grew between Jocelyn and Jon.

The Francis family gathered at the 120-year-old stone Cathedral of Our Merciful Saviour in Faribault, Minnesota. The church was filled to capacity with Easter worshippers. The Easter Vigil is the most ancient and beautiful of all Christian celebrations—a service resplendent with music, scripture, tradition, and the sacraments of baptism, confirmation, and Eucharist (Holy Communion).

Jonathan, dressed in white, was baptized with water and the Holy Spirit in the stone baptismal font by our priest and friend from Holy Cross Church in Dundas, the Reverend Jim Newman. John and Coralie, Jonathan's godparents; our daughters; and my mother, Millie (as all of us affectionately called her) stood with us as we reaffirmed our baptismal covenant and renounced evil. Near the stained-glass window of Jesus the Good Shepherd, holding a lamb, Jonathan was anointed with oil and sealed by the Holy Spirit—marked as Christ's own forever.

Jocelyn was confirmed that evening. The bishop placed his hands on her head, passing down the ancient Christian sacrament of initiation into the assembly of the faithful. We received communion, celebrating the memorial of our redemption, recalling Christ's death, and proclaiming his resurrection and ascension. The Easter Vigil lasted for over three hours. Millie, a Baptist, turned to me several times during the service to ask, "Is it over yet?"

Jonathan's life in the Spirit was planted on that day. When, at age two, he and Linda walked past the Cathedral where he had been baptized, he looked up at the impressive building and said, "Look! It's King Friday's castle!" (from *Mr. Roger's Neighborhood*).

"No, Jonathan, that's the church where you were baptized," his mother replied.

"With water and the Holy Spirit!" he responded confidently.

The next year we had a daughter in college and a son in diapers. One of my favorite roles was "bath-giver." When I gave Jonathan his baths, we played with Biblical bathtub toys: Noah's Ark, and Jonah and the Whale.

I enjoyed Dr. Seuss books as much as Jonathan did. Among our favorite bedtime stories were the Jibboo, from *Oh! The Thinks You Can*

Think!, and *The Lorax*. *The Lorax* spoke for the trees and his voice spoke directly to Jonathan. He especially loved *Oh, the Places You'll Go!*

One day when four-year-old Jonathan and I were home alone, I made "ants on a log" for lunch. Linda had introduced me to this combination during her years in Girl Scout leadership.

I spread peanut butter on pieces of celery and topped them with raisins.

During our lunch, Jon turned to me and asked, "Dad, you're not supposed to put raisins up your nose, are you?"

"No, Jonathan. Do you have a raisin in your nose?" I asked.

"Yes," he replied in a trusting tone that said simply, *Hey, Dad, we have a problem.*

Jonathan remained perfectly still as I held a flashlight and painlessly removed the raisin with a pair of tweezers.

At five, Jonathan wanted to help make our favorite chocolate chip cookies with me. He stood on a chair to see as I mixed the ingredients. Jonathan asked to break the egg. Half of the raw egg went on the floor. We baked the cookies anyway with only half an egg, but they turned out as hard as hockey pucks. So, Jonathan and I mixed up a new batch. Again, he wanted to add the egg. Again, half went on the floor. So, I

So be sure when you step.
Step with care and great tact
And remember that Life's a great balancing act.
Just never forget to be dexterous and deft.
And never mix up your right foot with your left...

—from *Oh, the Places You'll Go!* by Dr. Seuss

added another egg to make an egg-and-a-half. This time, the cookies rose up, and we enjoyed delicious, chocolate chip muffins.

I asked, "Jonathan, what do you think is the most important ingredient in chocolate chip cookies?"

"I think it's the egg," he replied.

Linda and I were both forty-four years old when Jonathan started kindergarten. We attended the parents' orientation, and were clearly the oldest couple in the room. The teachers and the other parents looked young enough to be our children.

I stayed at home in the morning to take him to the school bus stop on his first day of kindergarten. But, before long Jonathan started going to the bus stop on his own. We watched as he raced the other neighborhood boys to see who could get to the bus stop first.

When Jonathan was a five-year-old soccer player his speed, tenacity, and competitive spirit were already obvious. He ran up and down the

WALKING JONATHAN TO THE BUS STOP FOR KINDERGARTEN

field chasing the ball faster than anyone else. His sisters had encouraged his physical coordination, holding dance parties with him from the time he could walk. The girls were athletes as well in either skating or soccer. In high school Jocelyn earned a varsity letter playing on the boys' soccer team.

When Jonathan was eight, he urged the whole family to play backyard touch football. We played it Minnesota style—in the snow in winter, and especially during Christmas vacation when his sisters and their significant others were home.

All three of our daughters had left home for college so we downsized. We moved from Northfield to our new country home built on three acres just north of Stillwater, Minnesota. We chose Stillwater because it's a great "village"—a small town of about 15,000 people, nestled in wooded hills in the scenic St. Croix River Valley.

Jonathan made the transition gracefully and immediately fell in love with his rural environment and his open school, Stonebridge Elementary. He thrived in the self-paced atmosphere. At Stonebridge, we witnessed the personal discipline, work ethic, integrity, and self-regulated behavior that became hallmarks of his character.

In his schoolwork, Jonathan wrote about his growing respect and reverence for the earth, God's Creation—the natural world. His first small acts of conservation became a unique and exciting opportunity for us to learn from our child. He taught us how to reduce, reuse, and recycle. He educated us about how lawn mower engines were major polluters. With his frequent encouragement I bought a battery powered, rechargeable lawn mower.

He brought home information about the environmental damage done by phosphates in lawn fertilizers. I learned from him about the use of corn gluten meal, an environmentally safe natural weed suppressant and fertilizer. It worked! Gently, persistently, our young son taught us how to be more environmentally sensitive and how to take positive action. We found and used organic and safe recipes for every purpose. We planted trees—more than fifty pine seedlings. However, our soil was so inert that few of them survived; but our apple tree flourished.

In that same year, Jonathan and I were introduced to the pristine Boundary Waters Canoe Area Wilderness (BWCAW) in Northern Minnesota. My friend Dave, along with his son Stephen, took us on our first Boundary Waters trip. The BWCAW covers more than a million acres, extending nearly 150 miles along the Canadian border, with more than 1,200 miles of canoe routes and 2,000 campsites. Great glaciers left behind rugged cliffs and crags, canyons, gentle hills, towering rock formations, rocky shores, sandy beaches, and several thousand lakes and streams. The nearest mountain range is the Sawtooth Mountains, which rise from Lake Superior. Like the range in Idaho, I suspected that they received their name because they resemble the teeth of an immense saw.

Jonathan, at four foot, six inches tall and sixty pounds, bravely did his best to help me carry our one-hundred-pound aluminum canoe through a portage. While paddling and looking for a campsite, Jonathan and I were in the middle of a large lake, battling high winds and choppy waters. Jonathan, in front, struggled to keep us on course. I was proud of my young son's tenacious grit.

When Jonathan caught a twelve-inch northern pike, a bony fish we decided not to eat, he built a stone pond in the lake for the fish and watched it swim around for a few hours before releasing it back into the deep water. That summer, I witnessed Jonathan's true love and respect for nature.

He and I made several trips together to the Boundary Waters, often on Father's Day weekend. Jon teased before each departure, "Dad, have you over-packed yet for our camping trip?"

At twelve Jonathan had his own bank account and checkbook. His mother taught him how to balance a checking account and live within

DAVID AND JONATHAN IN MINNESOTA'S BOUNDARY WATERS CANOE AREA

a budget. He caught on, learning how to be frugal and responsible with his money and resources.

Jonathan spent hours by himself doing homework or building projects. He was always constructing something. One of his massive projects, an entire city, covered half of his basement play area, with buildings, roads, stores, houses—even a power plant.

At the dinner table one evening, thirteen-year-old Jonathan announced that he didn't want to be called Jonathan anymore. His name would be Jon.

From then on we called him Jon, most of the time.

During six of the nine years that Jon played soccer, I was his coach. Jon handled it gracefully. We traveled to tournaments all over Minnesota and in several other states. One season, his team, the Red Devils, took me to the Minnesota State Soccer Tournament. The team wore

THE RED DEVILS (JON FAR LEFT, COACH-DAD IN SUNGLASSES)

red and black jerseys—the school colors of the Stillwater High School Ponies. The Red Devils were an awesome team. They displayed spirit, determination, and teamwork.

Jon demonstrated an outstanding ability to stop his opponent's forward progress. Although he wanted to play an offensive position, I placed him in defense where he would have more success, and he didn't argue with me. As his coach, I noticed that he rarely complained about or criticized others.

I had never played soccer, so I worked hard to be a good coach. At fifty, I attended several weeks of coach's school at the National Sport's Center in Blaine, Minnesota, and earned my D License. I triumphantly presented my certificate to Jon.

"Hey, Jon," I said, "I passed, and I now qualify to coach soccer at the high school level."

He thought for a moment and responded, "Dad, that's a scary thought."

My years as Jonathan's coach were extraordinarily satisfying for me and Jon was patient and tolerant with his dad-coach. However, one day when he was fourteen, he gently encouraged me to retire from coaching. I took his advice, and retired with a winning record. The same year, Jon gave up soccer to concentrate on running. His legs were always in motion.

On a flat road runs the well-train'd runner.
He is lean and sinewy with muscular legs.
He is thinly clothed, he leans forward as he runs,
with lightly closed fists and arms partially rais'd.

"The Runner" by Walt Whitman

I watched Jonathan grow into an accomplished athlete. He saw me run competitively for many years and began to express interest. When he finished second at the Stonebridge one-mile in sixth grade, I sensed he had a gift. Our first race together, on July 4, 1993, was the Marine on St. Croix two-mile run. Jon was eleven. We ran side by side and finished together.

In eighth grade, Jon was one of the fastest runners in his class. His junior high coach, Shelly Christensen, was married to the high school track and cross country coach. Not unlike a minor league farm club, Shelly alerted her husband Scott to budding junior high talent and told him to keep an eye on that Francis kid.

In ninth grade, Jon was drafted for varsity track. Scott Christensen was an outstanding high school coach who nurtured Jon's natural talent and work ethic. He told us that genetics plays an important role in running ability. It's how people are wired, and Jon was wired to run. At five

FATHER AND SON AND A TWO-MILE RUN, JULY 4, 1993

foot, four inches, his running looked effortless with an efficient, classic stride. He ran outdoors throughout Minnesota's daunting winters.

As a fifteen-year-old high school sophomore, Jon earned a top spot on the high school's varsity boys cross country team and helped lead it to a state and national championship. The 1997 Stillwater High School Boys Cross Country Team went undefeated. They were Conference, Section, and State Champions and voted by the sports' writers (*USA Today/Harrier's*) as National Champions (ranked first out of 23,000 high school boys teams). Jon finished eighth at the sectional, completing the 5K course in 16:18, and qualifying for his first Minnesota State Meet. At the Minnesota State High School Cross Country Running Meet at St. Olaf College in Northfield, Jon was the fifteenth competitor and

THE MAGNIFICENT SEVEN: 1997 MINNESOTA STATE HIGH SCHOOL AND NATIONAL CHAMPIONS (LEFT TO RIGHT: COACH SCOTT CHRISTENSEN, SEAN GRAHAM, LUKE WATSON, GREG WIKELIUS, CHRIS BOLDT, JON FRANCIS, JOEL SOLOMONSON, AND PETE PRINCE)

the fourth Stillwater runner to cross the finish line. Jon earned All Conference and All State honors that year. This was a "three-peat" for Stillwater...their third consecutive Boys Cross Country Championship. Local sports writers dubbed them "The Magnificent Seven."

"You smell like a wet dog," Jocelyn said to Jon when he returned home after a run. The nickname stuck. The entire family started calling him Jon Dog.

The movie *Chariots of Fire* was Jon Dog's favorite movie. He watched it the night before every big race. *Chariots of Fire* tells the true story of Eric Liddell and Harold Abrahams, two men driven by the need to run. Both exhibited exceptional speed and trained passionately to compete in the 1924 Olympics. Eric Liddell, a Protestant missionary from Scotland, said he ran "for the glory of God." After winning Olympic medals in France, he traded glory and applause for an opportunity to preach the gospel. Running was also an expression of Jon's faith. He had a gift and, like Eric Liddell, he ran to glorify God. Inside Jon's CD of the soundtrack of *Chariots of Fire*, Jon wrote: "Where does the power come from to see the race to its end? From within."

When Jon was a senior in high school, Linda and I arrived at the sectional meet on a cold October afternoon. At the start, Jon moved to the front. He was out to run a personal best time and earn a spot at the State meet. His lead was so large it looked like he was running the race alone. Jon was "in the zone" and did not recognize that the golf cart driver took a wrong turn leading Jon and a handful of other runners on a 200-yard detour.

Jon regained the course, far behind, and ran a blistering pace to catch up and finish eleventh. Unfortunately, only the top ten finishers go to State. We, and all Stillwater fans, where outraged at what the incompetent cart driver "had done" to Jon.

But Jon said afterward, "No. It was my fault. I should have known the course better."

This example of Jon's character and good humor (along with his competitive spirit) were no doubt what Jon's peers recognized when Jon was elected captain of both his high school and college track and cross country teams. The running road trips were often long, but always enjoyable. We traveled all over the U.S. for track and cross country meets and races. In addition to his high school running, Jon competed in Foot Locker and Junior Olympics.

I had the pleasure of running several races with him. One spring morning, we rose early and ran a 10K together. Jon finished second. He was never able to pass the leader, an elite runner from Germany. (I finished around 200th.)

Waiting at the finish line, Jon greeted, "Hey Dad, I didn't expect you back so soon!"

One of Jon's most exciting races was the Gopher to Badger Half Marathon. I was standing near the finish line when spectators began to strain their necks to view the front runner, all by himself, coming down the road. "Who is that?" several asked.

"That's my son, Jon."

We returned to Northfield many times for races. Once, I stood on the football stadium field and watched in amazement as Jon ran the 2000 Meter Steeplechase, on the track at the 100th Annual Carleton College Invitational Track and Field Meet. Jon looked like a Marine running an obstacle course as he gracefully and powerfully leaped over the hurdles and the water. I had to restrain myself from running beside him. Jon won the event with a personal best time of 6:11.98.

Jon's close friend Kevin Doe had been Jon's teammate and running partner in high school. Both were talented runners, so they were grouped together in workouts. They had a tight-knit and respectful bond even though they were a year apart and had different circles of friends. Jon was shorter in stature; Kevin towered over him by a foot. Kevin was teased that Jon must be a better athlete because he had to take twice as many strides for every one Kevin took.

Kevin described the nature of their friendship:

Jon embodied loud, vocal leadership while I preferred to quietly lead by example. Jon envisioned bold changes; I felt content with the way things were. We seemed opposites in many respects, but our friendship began because of Jon's warm, outgoing character. He took the initiative to reach out and make friends with others. I became friends with Jon because of his remarkable ability to welcome outsiders into his friendship.

Jon at Carleton (1999)

While we were in high school, I had a unique experience that offered a glimpse into Jon's future. I invited him to meet at my house for a distance run on a Sunday afternoon. After the run, he wanted to know what I was doing that afternoon. I told him that I was going to Sunday night Mass. Jon said he wanted to come along. Surprised by this, I asked if he was serious. To most high schoolers, going to church was an activity done as part of a routine or enforced by their parents. Adding to my concern was the fact that Jon was not a Roman Catholic. But he assured me that he really wanted to go to church with me.

So, my mom and I attended Mass with Jon as our guest. He appeared at home there. He truly enjoyed himself and sang the hymns louder and with much more energy than everyone around him. He seemed excited to take it all in, to see how our faith was similar and different to his. This was a strong indicator to me that Jon's future would be based on sharing his faith with others.

Through our college years, I was able to see other examples of Jon putting his faith into action. It was inspiring for me to see this person who got such satisfaction and happiness from helping others, while most of my peers only received that satisfaction through their own personal gain. Most people in their twenties keep busy taking care of themselves, but Jon actually thought about taking care of others.

I often got postcards, handwritten letters, and emails from Jon, wherever he was, sometimes in the Western U.S. or South America. He always told interesting stories about his religious service and youth ministry, mostly happy stories. He did face some tough times, but he always remained positive and found some humor in the situation. Jon inspired me to keep in contact with my other friends. He always ended with, "Peace & Love, Jon," a closing message that no one else I knew ever used. But it was a message that Jon exemplified better than anyone else.

Jon's best friend and running partner at Augustana College was a journalism major who grew up in Sioux City, Iowa. Mike's parents became our good friends as we traveled the running circuit together. We often joked that Jon and Mike could spend hours together without saying a word, yet enjoy the experience. On Mike's twenty-second birthday, he was a little ornery because he had to get up for a six-thirty a.m. track workout. In came Jon wearing a homemade party hat, carrying cupcakes he had baked, and singing "Happy Birthday" to Mike.

Since Jon was on the five-year plan, pursuing three majors, Mike graduated from Augustana in 2004, a year earlier. He took a job as a reporter in Beatrice, Nebraska, and invited Jon to run the Lincoln Marathon with him on May 1, 2005. Linda and I drove to Sioux Falls, picked up our son, and took him to Lincoln.

Race day was chilly. As usual, Jon started fast and stayed in the top ten through mile sixteen. Mike chose a slower pace. When Jon became

2003 AUGUSTANA RUNNING TEAMS. JON IN FRONT (THIRD FROM RIGHT.) COACH TRACY HELLMAN (FAR RIGHT IN BACK).

chilled, he fell back. Mike caught up to him and stayed with Jon to the finish. Mike and Jon crossed the finish line side by side. The race results:

97 JON FRANCIS   SIOUX FALLS SD 23 M 3/36 3:12:55
98 MICHAEL GOODWIN   BEATRICE NE 23 M 4/36 3:12:55

Mike described the race:

The Lincoln Marathon was the first marathon finish for both of us. We hadn't planned to finish together. Jon thought he was in good shape and planned to go out fast. I had made the same mistake in a previous attempt at a marathon and ended up not finishing. With that in mind, I suggested to Jon that it might be prudent to

60

be more conservative at the beginning of the race. Jon, however, was stubborn and determined to stick to his plan.

I caught up to him at about mile twenty-two. I was miserable, but Jon was in worse shape. We were running into a stiff, cold wind, and Jon was only wearing a tank top and running shorts. The muscles in his legs were cramping up. We both stumbled along, alternately walking and jogging, until we finally reached the finish.

Although the marathon hadn't gone as either of us planned, it felt right to finish together. As teammates on a small cross country team at a small college, we had done hundreds of runs. It was fitting that we experienced that significant milestone together after having run together for so long.

After Jon crossed the finish line, we hugged each other. He was relieved and happy to have completed his first marathon, but unhappy with his time. Jon vowed that he would break three hours on his next one. Mike went on to qualify for and run the Boston Marathon.

We found Jon's tattered road atlas in his car in July 2006. He had marked the thirty-five states where he had either competed or trained. I will forever cherish those years—often in extreme cold, rain, heat, and humidity—watching Jon run with passion and joy. Jon's legs were kissed by God.

THE LINCOLN MARATHON (2005)

So Many Shoes
by David Francis

Jon's shoes.
So many shoes.
White Adidas,
Blue Nike,
Worn Cleats,
Asics—
His favorite.
Reminders of his gift.
Reminders of his passion.
Reminders of our loss.

Chapter 9

JOURNEY OF SORROW

Monday, August 7, 2006, Sawtooth City, Idaho

Leaving Idaho in August, Linda and I were unwilling pilgrims on a journey of sorrow. First, we returned to Luther Heights Bible Camp to gather Jon's belongings. We met again with staff and campers who were still in tears and shock. We attended chapel at the camp and ate dinner in the dining hall. I climbed to the highest point called the "Rock" where Jon had lingered many times. I sat, looked over the awesome landscape, and cried.

The cabins at Luther Heights Bible Camp were named after Idaho summits: Castle, Washington, Thompson, Horton, Braxon, Patterson, Blackman, Williams, and Hortsmann, etc. With friends from Luther Heights Camp, Jon had climbed most of them. Some he climbed more than once. Jon also gained the highest summit in Idaho, 12,655-foot Mount Borah in the White Cloud Mountains.

Perhaps like Moses, Abraham, and Jesus, Jon went up the mountain to seek God's mind. I can't be sure, but I do know that Jon believed the mountains throbbed with the heart of God.

We visited all of the camp places Jon had been, regarding them all as sacred spaces. Finally, we gathered Jon's belongings. In the sparse cabin where he had slept, we found his set of keys—to the house,

car, and church. Reverently, I buried my
nose in my son's clothing to inhale his
familiar fragrance. We packed his things
into his car, a green Subaru Outback he
had recently purchased—his first car.

Except for what he carried with him up
the Grand Mogul on July 15, 2006, Jon's
car now held everything he had taken with

JON ON TOP OF THOMPSON
PEAK (2005)

him to Idaho. At nightfall, we left Luther Heights for our drive to
Ogden, Utah, where Jon had been serving as director of youth ministry
at Ascension Lutheran Church.

TUESDAY, AUGUST 8, 2006, OGDEN, UTAH

Ogden was surrounded by mountains, forests, hiking trails, and water. I
could see why Jon loved living in Utah. I could imagine him canoeing,
kayaking, skiing, and mountain climbing in this outdoor mecca. Linda
and I had not met Jon's new congregation, his pastor, or the youth
group until we arrived in Ogden.

Jon had rented a room from one of Ascension's members. Joanna,
a computer programmer, was a middle-aged, gentle, and soft-spoken
single woman. She joined us for lunch. She told us how much she
appreciated Jon's presence in her home and enjoyed hiking, climbing,
and skiing with him.

On August 16, Ascension Lutheran held a memorial service for
Jon. We were told of similar prayer vigils for Jon being held in churches
across the country.

Pastor David Kiel spoke for the congregation, saying:

We are here today to give thanks to God for the life of Jonathan David Francis! Jon did not live for himself. He loved the Lord. We all knew that…we all saw that. His whole life was about loving and serving God by loving and serving God's people. That's why he worked at a Christian camp. That is why he served this congregation as our minister of youth. That is why he led groups of people to work at Habitat for Humanity and to serve those less fortunate at St. Anne's Center here in Ogden. That's why Jon was coming back to Ascension after being at camp this summer and having worked at camp at least four summers in a row. That is why Jon was planning on going to seminary in a year. He loved the Lord and he lived for the Lord.

Jon loved life! We saw it. We experienced it. His love for life made us all smile! And we all know that his love for life was grounded deeply in his love for God. Jon lived an abundant life—and it was abundant because he was a servant of Christ. It gave his life purpose and meaning. That's why Jon was so endearing to us. That's why we can thank God for him. That's why we can celebrate Jon this day in the midst of what we don't understand—in the midst of our sadness—in the midst of our loss.

Jon—we love you and we miss you deeply! Please know that you made a difference in our lives. Please know that you touched us all with the love of God. We will spend the rest of our lives in an attempt to honor you by serving each other just as you served us! We thank God for you and we'll carry you in our hearts always!

The people of Ascension shared our despair and disbelief. Linda and I were awash in the love and grief of Jon's congregation. We met with Jon's youth group in the room that they had painted in bright fluorescent colors and decorated with scripture. A shocking lime-green wall had "God Loves You" painted in large blue letters. The young people wore white ribbons with "Jon Francis" printed on them. The kids gave us balloons and cards with written notes to Jon, expressing their love for him and their anguish that they would never be able to see him again. For many of these kids, this was the first time in their lives that they had encountered a loss this painful—the unresolved loss of a teacher, mentor, and friend.

Behind tears and brave faces, they told stories about Jon. He was not much older than they were, but he lived an authentic, faith-filled life that they admired. He talked the talk and walked the walk. He brought fun and joy into their lives. The depth and strength of his ministry were evident. He told them about his faith and taught the gospel with deep conviction. He was real, and he was never boring.

They told stories of how competitive Jon could be on the playing field. I told them my own tale of how Jon tried to knock me out of our family football games, and how he roughhoused with his sisters. During our backyard football games, touch often turned into tackle. Jonathan preferred to play on the team opposing me so he could take occasional shots at me. During one game, he hit me so hard I flew horizontally through the air and landed five feet away. "Jon, if you do that again, you'll be grounded," his mother had shouted at her twenty-one-year-old son.

A youth leader told us how Jon helped organize the annual Ascension 5K Grace Race that spring. He finished first, set a new course record, and then circled back on the course to encourage other runners.

Several members of Ascension were mountain climbers, and some were search and rescue professionals. A few reminded me that they had been with us in Idaho in July and wanted to continue the search for Jon. I thanked them all, and we set a date in late August to meet in Stanley.

Next, Linda and I drove to Joanna's house. Packing up our son's personal belongings was a gut-wrenching experience. Our hands often shook as we touched, smelled, read, caressed, cried, and eventually placed in boxes Jon's clothing, letters, books, CDs, pictures, sports equipment, and his applications to seminaries. I found his registration and entry form for the November 2006 Seattle Marathon. I instantly knew why he picked Seattle for his second marathon. Alexis Nelson, his high school sweetheart, lived there.

We performed the same sorrowful task at Jon's office at the church. I found the laptop computer I gave him for college. But I could not bring myself to open it or look at any of his files.

We ran out of room inside Jon's Subaru, so we bought a car-top carrier, and Joanna rigged a makeshift bike carrier for Jon's mountain bike. We said goodbye, hugged Joanna, and thanked her for being a good friend to our son. Linda and I headed east toward Minnesota. When she drove, I sat in the passenger seat and cried. Then we switched, and it was her turn to cry. Late one day, while driving across Nebraska, we stopped for the night. We were in Lincoln where Jon ran a marathon in 2005. As I pulled off the Interstate, Linda and I both gasped immediately when we recognized the same hotel where we stayed with Jon. We had no tolerance at that moment for any reminders of good times with Jon. I circled around and drove on to the next exit.

When we arrived in Minnesota, our neighbors greeted us and helped us unload Jon's car. We neatly and carefully placed Jon's belongings in the garage. We needed time to decide where his things would be stored. Linda went upstairs and put the Ascension balloons and love notes in Jon's bedroom.

The following day, Linda and I began responding to the hundreds of cards, letters, phone messages, and donations. Our friend Shirley brought over dinner and copies of the St. Paul, Minneapolis, and Stillwater newspapers that contained articles on Jon's disappearance. I didn't realize until then the intense level of outrage that was felt by so many in Minnesota toward the Idaho officials in response to their decision to abruptly stop the search.

In the mail were several copies of *Lament for a Son* written by Nicholas Wolterstorff, professor of Theology at Yale Divinity School. Professor Wolterstorff's twenty-five-year-old son, Eric, died while mountain climbing alone in Austria. One of the copies was mailed from Spokane, Washington, by Bishop Martin Wells, Jon's Bishop. I opened the book and read a few pages.

Page 9 began, "The call came at 3:30 on that Sunday afternoon, a bright sunny day." I closed the book. I couldn't read any more. No! This couldn't be. Our call came at 3:15, on a Sunday afternoon, July 16, 2006, a bright sunny day.

Lament sat at my bedside for many days until I was able to open it again. When I did, I read, "There's a hole in the world now. In the place where he was, there's now just nothing.... The world is emptier. My son is gone. Only a hole remains, a void, a gap, never to be filled."

Someone else felt the same unbearable pain I was feeling, but was able to express it. Someone else experienced the agony of losing a young son. *Lament* is a beautiful love song from a father to his son who died too soon, too sadly, too suddenly.

After struggling through *Lament*, I had to force myself to place my despair onto a shelf somewhere. I did not have time to deal with my own anguish. I had to find Jon and bring him home!

Chapter 10

FINAL APPEAL

From the first day that we were abandoned by law enforcement, I had worked the phone and the Internet to find search and rescue—now, search and recovery—resources. People I reached usually said, "Sorry, we can't respond without authorization from the sheriff."

I wrote several letters to the Custer County sheriff, Custer County commissioners, and the Idaho governor. Since our meeting in July, we had not heard from the governor or his office. But the sheriff and I had exchanged letters. I naively believed that an appeal from us would gain some cooperation.

On August 22, I mailed this plea:

Dear Sheriff Eikens:

I request your renewed help in our search for our son Jon. We have not found him. This is a very painful and sorrowful situation for my wife, Linda, and me, and our family.

We pray, and we work to bring Jon down from the mountain. Jon is young, and his disappearance was unexpected. My family and I desperately need "closure" and the opportunity to end this stressful uncertainty, and to provide Jon with a proper burial.

I request your assistance in helping us locate Jon and bring him home to Minnesota. As you know, many of your neighboring mountain states devote time and resources to lengthy searches and body recovery efforts. We especially need certified recovery dogs. Let me know what obstacles lay in the path of official Idaho involvement:

- Funding? Jon's family and friends will help with this.
- Liability/Workman's Comp? The State of Minnesota has offered to partner with Idaho.

I am returning to Idaho this week to continue the search for our son. I am available to meet with you on Monday, August 28, or Tuesday, the 29, in Challis at your convenience.

I look forward to hearing from you.

Regards,

David Francis

Sheriff Eikens responded with more political "cover" and questionable logic about creating a precedent for a search lasting longer than three days. My final letter to him that year openly challenged his decision and his behavior.

Dear Sheriff Eikens:

Thank you for responding to my letter of August 22nd. This is a welcome dialogue. Allow me to respond appropriately to your positions and correct some of your misunderstandings.

You ended the search for our son because of exhausted resources?

As a result of my unwanted crash course in mountain search and rescue, I learned from countless experts that a two-day search on Grand Mogul was inadequate: "It was not an adequate effort."

The courageous volunteers were heartbroken when you ended the search after only two days.

We have since learned that search and recovery efforts in Minnesota and in your neighboring mountain states often last for fourteen days or more.

We are private citizens, not Idaho officials, and we were able to gather more capable search dogs and volunteers than you brought to bear.

The best way to prevent "eminent danger that courageous volunteers were exposed to" is to put expert search and rescue personnel on the mountain. When you hold authority, you also carry the responsibility. Because of your position, you had the ability to request and authorize those experts.

You did not utilize all of the available SAR resources you could have.

Political pressures were implemented by me?

Incorrect. The outpouring of support from Minnesota and across the country was spontaneous. It resulted from the affection for Jon and for my family from so many people — not political connections. Jon was a remarkable young man who touched hundreds of people in his brief life.

I was too busy organizing and interviewing volunteers and begging for search dogs. I am not an elected official in Minnesota and have no political influence.

The national outrage was the result of the great affection for Jon and your decision to abandon the search for him after only two days. Sadly this unwanted attention caused you to become defensive.

Redundant search effort?

I was present for most of your official search. The Custer County search stuck to known and safe routes as directed by the incident commander. Our volunteers went off trail and searched the more difficult and numerous unsearched areas.

It was 3 p.m. on Monday, July 17th, when I approached the IC and asked him if anyone had been to the summit to see if Jon had made it. At my urging, he asked for volunteers to go to the summit. Two from the Sawtooth Mountain Guides volunteered. It was 6 p.m., near the end of the first full day of the search, before you determined Jon's last known position and knew that Jon had gained the summit.

We put search dogs on the summit. The official search team did not. At the same time there was a body recovery effort underway in the mountains of Utah using expert SAR resources that went for eight days.

We have put over two hundred searchers on the mountain and brought all of them back safely.

Political precedent?

It is disturbing that you are "disturbed" by the use of all available resources to find missing people in your jurisdiction. The military aircraft were of questionable value, and used mainly for State of Idaho political cover.

We were optimistic when we heard that the governor and his wife were coming to visit with us, and hopeful that he would add State resources to the search. The meeting was a crushing disappointment. It was obvious that you had briefed Governor Risch, and that he was on message and came only to warn us about risking other people in our search for our son.

You know as well as I do that the best way to minimize risk in a search is to use expert, trained resources under official control.

You made the conscious decision not to assume any additional liability or expense in the search for my son. Remember, along with your authority comes a responsibility to serve others.

Future cooperation?

I cannot tell you how disappointed I am by the reluctance of the State of Idaho to cooperate with us in our recovery efforts. Since July 16 we have had many missed opportunities to collaborate in sharing expenses, liability, and risk. This has added to our deep grief.

The loss of a child is the deepest and most long-lasting sorrow known to humanity. Grief upon grief is added because we are not able to recover our son's remains and give him a proper and respectful burial.

Finally, unless you have lost a child in an early, sudden, and unexplained accident, please do not lecture me about acceptance. We and others will return again and again to Idaho until we find Jon Francis. When we do, I will call you to assist us in carrying his remains off the Grand Mogul.

Respectfully,

David Francis

CC: Governor James Risch

When Jocelyn requested and received the official Custer County search documents, we also received the message log written by the sheriff's office dispatcher that displayed their defensive and misguided attitudes.

7-31-06...200 (CCS) spoke with [two Minnesota political officials] and told them both that this all started politically and needed to end politically and that their respective offices needed to work together to quash this.

07-18-06...Our search and rescue members searched and then
Mr. Francis' father pulled some political strings and we also had
the National Guard here to search.

The sheriff was wrong again. The call to the Minnesota governor's office was made by Erin Ghere, Jon's close friend from Ascension Episcopal Church in Stillwater. Erin and Jon spent many years together in the Ascension Youth Group and Teens Encounter Christ (TEC). Erin's brother Chris had traveled alongside Jon on their common faith journey. He worked tirelessly during the week Jon was reported missing and, along with Father Jerry, fielded hundreds of phone calls, collected money for the search, and organized search parties and caravans to Idaho. Chris had arranged for our first handler and search dog, Jim Hanley and Shania.

Reaching out to and debating with public officials was clearly a waste of my time. I needed to focus my attention on our effort to recover Jon's remains. I was not willing to give up my son to the mountain.

Chapter 11

THE MIGHTY ASCENSION SEARCH TEAM

In the third week of August 2006, I returned to Idaho. Linda did not go with me. She said she could not bear "to look at that mountain again."

As planned, I joined up with the team from Ascension Lutheran and several other volunteers in Stanley. On August 24, we set up a well-stocked campsite at the Inlet Transfer Camp on the Shore of Redfish Lake near the trailhead to the Grand Mogul. Assembled there were four members of the Sawtooth Mountain Guides, fourteen fit and experienced mountaineers from Jon's church in Ogden, our search manager Jeff Hasse, and me.

The group that came from Ascension later became known as "The Mighty Ascension Search Team." They were Jon's friends and fellow parishioners—all were lean, solid, experienced climbers—probably the most capable search team ever to climb the Grand Mogul. While at home in Minnesota, I purchased my first pair of real hiking boots and pants. I would no longer climb in blue jeans and running shoes.

Jon and I loved to go camping. Together we had enjoyed the sights and smells of the wilderness. But now, I was numb to those sensations. On Redfish Lake, my nostrils inhaled the odor of pine trees that should have been cleansing and healing. The view of the lake and mountains, the evening campfires, with the restful aroma and the hypnotic flames of burning wood, brought no peace. Even the camaraderie of Jon's friends from Ogden didn't comfort me. It was an out-of-focus movie. I was there for only one reason: to search that ugly mountain for my son.

Jeff Hasse had a search plan with supporting documents and maps. The plan included Jon's subject profile. This profile proved to be one of our best sources of clues. Ken Schulte, an experienced search and rescue professional, acted as assistant leader. We had advanced to a new level. We all carried handheld global positioning systems (GPS).

At 6,500 feet on the shores of Redfish Lake, the temperature dropped below freezing at night. It swung from thirty degrees Fahrenheit at breakfast to eighty degrees Fahrenheit during the heat of the day! In the early morning, I was uncomfortably cold. I quickly piled on layers of clothes. I shed the layers throughout the day as the sun warmed the thin, dry mountain air.

In the evening, our GPS tracks were downloaded onto Jeff and Ken's laptops to document areas that had been covered, and to help identify future search objectives. Like an Etch-A-Sketch, Jeff populated the electronic map of the mountain with thin, colored lines showing each person's route. We incessantly hovered over multiple maps—Jon's possible descent routes, previous search areas, and a map covered with numbered grids that marked all possible search quadrants. We were a professional, well-led search operation. Confidence and spirits were high.

For four days, we received our morning briefing and mission assignments from Jeff. I invited everyone to form a prayer circle to petition God for safety and success. Finally, I distributed string cheese from the large box I'd purchased at the Mountain Village Merc. This group of motivated, physically fit, experienced mountaineers set out for ten to twelve hours of hiking, climbing, and searching. When we returned to camp at the end of the day, there was always a hot supper prepared by the Mighty Ascension Camp Keepers.

The Mighty Ascension Team retraced Jon's ascent route up the avalanche field into the scree of the northeast ridge, up through the boulders and spires of granite onto the summit block and onto the 9,733-foot peak. Team members made entries in the summit log, declaring that they were in search of Jon Francis, whose last known position was at the summit on the morning of July 15, 2006.

In addition to the Ascension ground team, we had several capable dog teams—Jim Hanley and canine Shania, Danny Ibison and canine Tyler from Florida, and Johnny Unser Jr. and his dog Taz. This was Johnny's fourth mission. Johnny, the son of the late auto racer Johnny Unser—a tall, well-mannered gentleman—was a pleasure to work with. Jon's Idaho friends, Heather and Jordan Dale, worked with me, sweeping back and forth in a large boulder field on the east face. I joined the Mighty Ascension Search Team for a rugged, exhausting grid search of the east side of the Grand Mogul, traveling from north to south, all the way down into the surrounding forest, moving east to the forest service trail and beyond. We were pursuing one of the multiple, possible scenarios—that Jon may have wandered into the forest. Perhaps he had injured his head, was dazed or lost.

We started out in the morning, hiking single-file up the Forest Service Switch Back Trail, a relatively easy, well-marked, and heavily traveled trail that gained us 1,500 vertical feet to about 8,000 foot elevation. The Forest Service Trail (FST) is one of the "safe and prescribed routes" that Jon didn't take. Next, we traversed back and forth down the steep ridge into the forest drainage area. Descending the steep thirty- to forty-degree ridge, we surrendered 500 feet of our hard-earned climb so we could bushwhack through the forest to the eastern base of the Grand Mogul. We pushed through thick bushes, stepped over fallen trees, and crossed several flowing creeks to get to the granite boulders and scree areas of the Grand Mogul. I concluded that there were as many dead trees on the forest floor as there were standing lodgepole pines.

Twice I slipped into a creek. I lost two radios that day—both of them fell in the water. I cut my hand while clinging to an alder branch as I was falling. I was tired, wet, muddy, and bleeding. I didn't have the foresight to put my wallet in a waterproof container, so my wallet got wet, including pictures of my children and grandchildren.

We achieved a high POD (probability of detection) on the east side that week and were beginning to understand where Jon was not. Jeff summarized the late August missions in his expanding search log. After the evening software reconstruction was completed, we talked around the campfire and asked ourselves what the earlier search dog clues meant, and which of the six or seven possible descent routes Jon had chosen. After four exhausting days of searching, the time came for the Mighty Ascension Search Team to return to Utah, to their careers and families. They vowed to come back to Idaho and search again. As I said thank you and goodbye, I read the sadness and disappointment on their faces. I fell once more into a canyon of despondency. Bruce confessed to me that they had begun the week supremely confident they would find Jon.

Feeling defeated, I flew back to Minnesota to work with Jeff on planning and organizing our next search effort in September, and help Linda prepare for Jon's memorial service on September 9—"A Celebration of the Life and Ministry of Jon Francis."

THE MIGHTY ASCENSION SEARCH TEAM (FROM LEFT TO RIGHT, IN FRONT:
ERIC ENGELBY, BRUCE ENGELBY, KEN SCHULTE; BACK ROW: STUART SCHULTZ,
JEFF TURNER, CECILIA WEST, AND MIKE OTTO)

Chapter 12

A CELEBRATION OF LIFE

*"Jonathan; greatly beloved were you to me; your love to me
was wonderful…"*

2 SAMUEL 1:26 (NRSV)

Throughout the late summer of 2006, people asked us about our plans
for a service for Jon. They wanted to join as a community in grief and
pay their respects to him. Some asked if we were planning a funeral. I
explained that, in our tradition, a funeral required a body. Jon was missing and we couldn't find him. Maybe we never would. To me, Jon was
his body. Jon was the handsome face I had kissed again and again for so
many years, his own distinctive odor, and his curly, dark hair—the envy
of his mother. I would never again hug Jon's lean, athletic body. He was
lost, and my confidence was fading that we could ever bring him home.
So we planned a memorial service.

Several weeks after Jon went missing, the Francis family met with
our priest, Father Jerry, to create a service with as much joy and celebration as we could muster. We worked hard to put on brave faces and have
a public ceremony that reflected the love and joy Jon brought into the
lives of all who knew him. The service was meant to honor Jon's ministry and his commitment to share his faith as a teacher and a friend.

On Saturday, September 9, we held a "Celebration of the Life and Ministry of Jon Francis" at Ascension Episcopal Church in Stillwater. It was our church, the church where Jon grew up, the church that had a significant impact on the formation of his faith.

I wanted to give a talk, a tribute, a eulogy for my son. The day before the service, I stood in the pulpit and practiced reading it six times before I was able to get through it without crying.

Jon's celebration brought many of our cousins to Minnesota from across the country. Jon's teammates, coaches, and classmates from high school and college attended. Our three daughters and five grandchildren sat in the front pew alongside Linda and me. Jocelyn wore Jon's purple high school prom tuxedo in tribute.

My only sister, Juleen, came from Florida. Alexis Nelson, Jon's high school sweetheart, and her family sat with us. Don and Sally Caldwell, our dear friends but more like grandparents to Jon, sat close by.

Laura Aase and Eric Olsen came from Luther Heights Camp. As part of the service, Laura played guitar and sang "Arms of Love"—a favorite of Jon's. Our friends, Al and Carol Anderson, the first to learn that Linda was expecting Jon, and the first people I called from the Sawtooths in Idaho, joined us. Patty Wetterling was present. We were surrounded in love by more than 500 mourners—friends from Ascension Church in Stillwater, relatives, neighbors, and many friends from community, politics, and business.

A Eulogy for My Son, Jon

We should not be here today. This should not be happening to us. Children should bury their parents.

But we ARE HERE to celebrate the brief life and ministry of Jon Francis. We thank you for gathering to remember our son, to mourn his loss, and to celebrate his life.

Since my family and I began our journey of sorrow many weeks ago, dozens of people have spoken to us and said, "You raised an awesome son." Jon touched us. Jon was a man of strong character, deep faith, humility, patience, fun, adventure, and unconditional love.

I have thanked so many people for their kind words and responded, "His mother did a fine job, didn't she?" Jon's mother, Linda, and I fell in love many years ago. And we often spoke about a time when we would be married, have children together, and raise a family.

In high school, we picked out our children's names. We agreed that our first-born son would be named Jonathan David Francis. Jonathan and David, two strong, Old Testament names. I remembered from my Sunday school days that Jonathan loved David. (I Samuel, 18) "And it came to pass... that the soul of Jonathan was knit with the soul of David and Jonathan loved him as his own soul."

A part of my soul has been torn away. There is a hole in my heart. There is a big void in my family.

Since July 15 I have learned a great deal about mountain search and rescue, and about grief and loss. Here are some things I have learned:

The loss of a child is the deepest and most long-lasting sorrow known to humanity.

We've not only lost our son, but also his future. We've lost not only Jon's physical body, but also his dreams, his accomplishments. I cannot ignore, avoid, or go around the sorrow of my loss. I have to work through it. Help me in my grief. Tell me stories about Jon. Don't ask me questions I can't answer.

It was not God's will. Whatever happened on that mountain was not God's will. It was a terrible and tragic accident. God does not will death. God wants us to live. I believe that God shares our sorrow today.

God's promise of Eternal Life is wonderful. But, today, I would rather have the promise of hugging my son on his twenty-fifth birthday.

Closure is a myth. Closure is for bank accounts—not for love accounts. I know that I will have a love account with Jon my entire life.

Our son Jon was patient. For six years, he patiently put up with me as his soccer coach. When Jon was fourteen he said, "Dad, you're going to retire next year, right?" I said, "Yes, Jon, it's time for me to retire."

Our son Jon was humble. When he was a sophomore in high school, he ran varsity cross country. His team had an awesome year. They were undefeated, won the state championship, and were voted national champion high school boys cross country team.

Jostens created a super-bowl–style ring for the team. Jon would not order a ring. We encouraged him to buy one, but Jon said, "Dad, I don't need a ring. I know what we did." Touching his heart, he said, "I carry it in here."

Our son Jon was a man of deep faith. Jon's faith formation was supported by this church, its strong youth ministry, and Jon's experience in TEC.

When Jon was in high school, he and the Ascension Youth Group worked at a homeless shelter for children in Minneapolis. Many of the children were abandoned and abused. At the end of the service week, our priest came to us and said, "Your son Jon has a real gift for ministry to children."

We were pleased to see Jon live his ministry through high school, college, and after graduation.

When we stopped to gather Jon's belongings at Ascension Lutheran church in Ogden, where Jon was youth director, many members thanked us and told us how Jon had touched their lives. I asked several people how he did in his first job out of college. They said Jon was awesome. He was a blessing and a gift.

His mentor at Ascension Lutheran, Pastor David Kiel, told me that Jon had a down-to-earth, genuine ministry. He met the kids where they were, and brought fun and joy to his ministry. He attracted others by living an authentic, faith-filled life.

When my family and our friend and priest, Father Jerry, gathered at the base of the mountain in Idaho that Jon had climbed, Jon's sisters reminded us that Jon found a way to live above the pride and pettiness that afflict many of us. Jon was seldom mean-spirited, complaining, or petty. Jon seemed to see the best in everyone.

Jon got it! He loved life. And he loved people. He loved deeply and was deeply loved. Jon knew that we were not placed on earth to grab all of the objects, money, and status we can. We are born into this world to make a difference, to love God, and to love and serve others.

Jon got it!

I believe in my heart that Jon saw the world as God's wonderful creation. And the beautiful, natural world that God created cried out for protection and preservation. Jon saw all of the creatures in the world as God's creatures, worthy of respect. And Jon saw ALL PEOPLE as God's children, worthy of unconditional love.

That is how Jon Francis lived his life.

I know that Jon ran long distances and climbed mountains to challenge himself; but more importantly, he did those things to glorify God. Climbing mountains was a spiritual experience for him. I know Jon felt close to God at the summit.

Jon left a note in the summit registry on Grand Mogul. It reads, "07/15/06. Jon Francis, *LHBC [Luther Heights Bible Camp] and Ogden, Utah. Climbed avalanche field to east face and east ridge. Great times bouldering! All Glory to God for the climb and the beautiful Sawtooths."

Jon called home the week before he climbed the Grand Mogul. That was the last time I spoke with my son. He said, "Dad, I know you would like me to be in Minnesota and closer to home, but my ministry is out here." I said, "Jon, I know. It's called leaving home. It's all right. We all leave home."

I am grateful to God that I was given the opportunity to give Jon my blessing, and to say to him, "It's all right, son. It's called leaving home."

Finally, I am most grateful to God for giving us such as a remarkable son—for giving us the gift of Jon.

A long reception line extended from the church to the parish hall where Linda and I greeted hundreds of sad faces. We thanked them for coming and for remembering Jon. One after another those who knew and loved Jon expressed their sympathy and told us how much their lives had been touched by his. At a time when I felt abandoned by God, I saw God in the faces of hundreds of others who encircled us to help us bear our suffering.

Chapter 13

SNOW AND ICE

By late September, winter was closing in on the Sawtooths. Above the tree line, the Grand Mogul was ice-and-snow-covered. We needed to get back on the mountain before it became unsafe for people and dogs. Our primary September objective was to search from the summit east to the forest service trail. Paula McCollum and canine Jeb from Treasure Valley Search Dogs of Boise were with us. This was their fifth search mission. Janet Wilts and canine Chay-da from High Country K-9s in Wyoming joined us for their third mission. Paula and Janet and their dogs always raised our morale.

Ours was a mixed team from several states. In addition to Janet and Paula, we had Bill and Lois Hall from Iowa with their German shepherds, Hawk and Trax. Bill and Lois Hall, genuinely warm and sincere, were the complete search package, except for one thing: They had no mountain-climbing

Holding
by Jon Francis

The air is waiting,
winter is coming.
The ground exposed, barren,
ice covers and retreats.
We are made to be
patient, holding.

experience. However, they were hard working, highly trained, certified, and professional, and they had law enforcement experience and top credentials. Bill and Lois, self-admitted lowlanders from Iowa, were assigned trail searches that did not require mountain-climbing skills.

Jeff Hasse and I were joined by my son-in-law Steve, who was at my side on every search, and our friend Phil Alban, an avid outdoorsman, game hunter, and shameless optimist from Minnesota. On Friday, September 22, we had one of our best mixed canine teams working on the east side of the Grand Mogul. That day, Bill Hall recorded the weather in his report: "Temperatures ranged from 20-55 degrees F with winds from the northeast and variable 0-3MPH. Snow-covered at higher elevations and patches of snow at lower altitudes. 50-100% cloud cover."

Ryan, Lincoln, and Marc, all from The Sawtooth Mountain Guides, ascended to the northeast ridge, using the Lopez Route, and came down the same way. They missed the avalanche field on the descent and were suckered off-route into the toe of the ridge, which terminates in several loose steep gullies. I was part of a limited grid search of Outside Chance Valley along with Steve, Phil, and Rick Fahey, a local from Hailey, Idaho.

After six hours of climbing, we stopped at 8,600 feet. Just ahead was a breathtaking, snow-covered alpine valley. But we needed to turn around and get back to camp before nightfall. At the end of this vigorous effort, it became even more apparent that Jon would not be found on the east side of the Grand Mogul. He was certainly not in the forest and probably not on the eastern side of the summit block. Once again, I said thank you and goodbye to yet another team of dedicated volunteers. They had safely searched slippery terrain and bravely tolerated uncomfortably cold conditions.

Linda, Jeff, Steve, and I stayed at the Mountain Village Lodge in Stanley to organize and greet the next search team to climb on the last day in September. On Friday, September 29, we met with Ron Boswell and Twila York of Big Sky Search Dogs of Montana, and their German Shepherds, Mahto and Kona. Ron and Twila, a warm and loving couple, frequently enfolded Linda and me in their arms. We welcomed several returning members of the Mighty Ascension Search Team and Carren Corcoran and K-9 Cleo of Canine Search Solutions of Wisconsin. Carren stood out in the crowd with her flaming red hair.

Our next objective was the toe of the Grand Mogul, the area on the northeast that sloped down from the summit block into the forest. The weather now was similar to November in Minnesota. It was too cold to camp out overnight, so we provided motel rooms for the search teams and took the shuttle boat over to the trailhead. Normally, the Redfish Lake shuttle would be shut down by then; but Jeff, owner of the lodge, kept a boat in operation for us. We were joined by many faithful Idaho mountaineers.

The search plan had us shifting to the north side of the Grand Mogul, working primarily in the forest and drainage areas below the north face, and concentrating on the "toe." During Twila's search with her canine Kona, she fearlessly worked high on a cliff face and got "cliffed out." She could go no farther. Ron went up to help her down while I stayed with Mahto and tried my hand at giving dog commands. Mahto responded to the few canine search commands I had learned.

Jeff and I acted as support to Carren Corcoran and her Human Remains Detection (HRD) dog Cleo. The job of support personnel is to keep the handler safe. The handler is intent on working with the dog and interpreting the canine's signals. Support maintains position and clues and keeps the handler from walking off a cliff.

Dogs have a sense of smell many times greater than that of humans, and the best search dogs work hard and play hard. Certified HRD dogs, too often called cadaver dogs, train for months finding trace quantities of human scent. When they make a find, they are rewarded. I asked Carren to tell me about Cleo's training.

She explained that the average training for an HRD dog takes about eighteen months to get to an entry level of searching. Cleo was trained initially in basic human remains detection. Then Carren shrank down the size of remains to trace amounts—for crime-scene work. That type of work takes another one to two years. Human remains detection dogs are trained to detect the odor of actively decomposing or decomposed human remains. During life we all have a distinct or personal odor, and that is how a trailing dog trails a specific person. Upon biological death we humans immediately begin to decompose. Our remains pass into a "generic" human remains odor, which is vastly different than animal remains. Science has determined that human remains have more than 420 chemical signature odors. Animal remains have a different chemical makeup. A properly trained Human Remains detection dog is able to accurately distinguish between human and animal remains.

While searching for Jon, Carren told Jeff Hasse that, due to her trace work, Cleo was able to detect human remains farther away from source than an average HRD dog.

Cleo worked an area below the toe and created a classic scent cone, meaning that Cleo was detecting human odor. Cleo's recorded "hits" (the times she smelled the odor) created the shape of a cone. The point of the cone indicated the location of the human odor.

Carren wrote in her report, "At approximately eleven a.m., K9 Cleo, Jeff Hasse, and I entered a search area located on the north face of the mountain. K9 Cleo provided several formal indications, via a

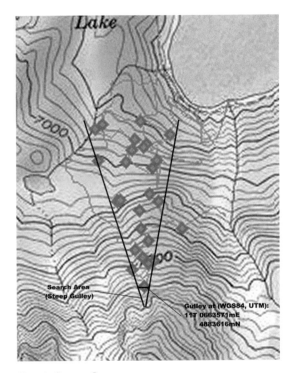

CLEO'S SCENT CONE

bark, that she detected the odor of human remains." Cleo led us up to a very steep talus slope (decaying granite, larger than scree) that turned out to be impossible for the dog or for us to climb.

I climbed up as far as I could but kept slipping back. We did not locate the source of the human odor. After dozens and dozens of search dog missions, Cleo's scent cone was the most compelling clue so far. We were all encouraged by Cleo's success, which directed our next mission to follow up and go higher on the north face. In addition to the three canine teams, we had two ground teams. Team 1, made up primarily of Mighty Ascension Search Team climbers, searched high. Team 2, the lowlanders, searched in the forest. The lowlanders included my wife Linda and our daughters Jocelyn and Melissa.

Snow, ice, and below-freezing temperatures dominated the Sawtooths by the beginning of October. Within a few weeks, the Grand Mogul would be frozen in the grip of winter. Despite adverse conditions, the search for Jon continued. On Friday, October 6, five members of the Sawtooth Mountain Guides followed up on the canine clues and searched the gullies on the toe of the ridgeline. This required rappelling into steep terrain. Nothing was found. On October 12, Sean Duffy, who had participated in several previous missions, set out on his own to follow up on Cleo's clues. In one day, Sean covered the entire northeast ridge from 8,500 to 9,100 feet.

The last search for Jon in 2006 was completed on the weekend of October 20–22. Probably this mission should never have taken place. The Grand Mogul was ice-and-snow-covered, and the temperatures were frigid. We agonized over this one. However, when we received commitments from some of the most skillful and experienced technical climbers, we gave this last-gasp effort a cautious green light. Linda and I remained in Minnesota. Doug and Jocelyn represented the family on the search and oversaw logistics. Peter Madsen, from Ketchum, opened up his cabin near Stanley to house most of the climbers.

Annie Williams, from the Smiley Creek Café, housed some of the searchers and dogs in her condo in Stanley. Annie is a member of "the club." She buried one of her children. Her twenty-five-year-old son Lane died in an accident in Idaho on July 13, 1992. Lane Jon Williams is buried in a cemetery in Ketchum, Idaho, near the grave of Ernest Hemingway.

We borrowed a boat from a volunteer in Hailey, Idaho, and Erik Leidecker hauled it to Redfish Lake using his father's truck. The winter team was composed of experienced technical climbers from Washington State, Minnesota, Idaho, and members of the Mighty Ascension Search Team. Paula McCollum and Jeb were the lone canine resource. This was an extremely well-planned and executed effort. The fact that we sustained no injuries of any kind that weekend is a testament to Jeff's leadership, good planning, and the skills of the climbers who went up on the mountain.

The primary mission objective was to search the area above Cleo's scent cone. This placed the searchers in the bowl below the Chockstone Couloir, nicknamed the "Boy Scout Couloir" after a group of stranded Boys Scouts were rescued there. Couloir is a French word, meaning deep mountain gorge or gully. This couloir on the north side of the Grand Mogul contained a huge boulder, an obstacle blocking the climbers' route. Jeff directed the missions on the north face and compiled the now-routine search summaries and GPS tracks.

On Saturday, October 21, Ground Team 2, Jeff Hasse and Ralph Katieb, worked in the bowl below the Chockstone Couloir and detected a smell of decomposition. Jeff gingerly probed into a nearby animal den but did not pick up any scent. The next day, Jeff and Ralph guided Paula and canine Jeb into the area where the odor was detected, but Jeb did not alert. The source was not found.

Snow and ice conditions were too dangerous to safely move on the slippery granite by late Sunday, forcing the search for Jon to be discontinued. The October searches had been risky and disappointing.

Since July, we had searched for thirty-five days with 114 search teams, 391 searcher days, fifty canine searcher days, and eighteen different certified search dogs—a significant achievement. We had spent over forty thousand dollars and assembled a lengthy clue log. But we did not find Jon.

I felt guilt and remorse that I had not worked smart enough or hard enough to find our son. I failed to find Jon and bring him off that mountain. I didn't participate in any of the searches after the first of October. I was not on the icy mountain and never smelled the odor of decomposition. Instead I had returned home on October 2 to finish my campaign for the Minnesota State Senate.

SEARCH MANAGER, JEFF HASSE (RIGHT), ON LAST SEARCH IN 2006

Chapter 14

THE CAMPAIGN

The first time Jon met my friend Paul Wellstone, Jon was eight and we were carrying our fishing poles near the Carleton College stadium, in Northfield, located on the bank of the Cannon River. Paul was a professor at Carleton at the time and he was working out near the stadium. I introduced Jon to Professor Wellstone. Jon was polite but far more eager to start fishing on that day.

Paul and I and many of his colleagues ran long distances together back then. Paul could run and talk passionately about politics at the same time. I usually struggled to keep pace and just listened and learned.

Several years later, when Jon was a teenager on his way to a running camp in Colorado, we crossed paths with now Senator Wellstone at the Twin Cities airport. This time, Jon complimented the senator for his concern and advocacy for the environment.

Paul Wellstone, a populist leader and engaging spokesman for progressive values, served in the U.S. Senate from 1991 until his death in a plane crash, along with his wife Sheila and daughter Marcia, in Northern Minnesota on October 25, 2002, eleven days before the midterm election. I continue to be inspired by his life and his legacy. My favorite Wellstone wisdom, from his book, *The Conscience of a Liberal*, is, "We all do better, when we all do better."

In June 2005, I graduated from Camp Wellstone, an excellent weekend training session teaching grassroots political organization. There, I was reminded that "liberal" is not a four-letter word. The United States was founded on liberal principles: belonging to the people, advocating personal freedom, freedom from rigid doctrine, gradual reform in political and social institutions.

When I decided to run for the Minnesota State Senate in the 2006 election, I called Jon at his college in South Dakota to let him know. As usual for Jon, he thought for a moment before offering his opinion. "Dad," he asked, "can't you find another way to make a difference?"

Jon and I shared a passion for social justice, but he had little interest in political involvement. Jon expressed his belief that people can make a contribution to the world in many other ways. I defended my decision by saying that the political process was an excellent way to change things for the better. We agreed to disagree.

I was disappointed that I didn't have Jon's enthusiastic support. I had hoped he might come home for the summer and work on my campaign. I would have enjoyed his companionship and the humorous barbs he often laid on me to keep me humble.

I was seeking public office because years of conservative-dominated politics had blocked Minnesota's forward movement. I wanted to return our state to a place of national leadership in education, healthcare, and economic competitiveness.

I grew up in Michigan in a low-income Irish, Protestant, republican family—an unusual combination. I knew diversity and scarcity, and learned tolerance and compassion. President Kennedy had inspired me and challenged my generation to serve and to make a difference. We had the ability and, yes, the obligation to make things better. Politics was part of the solution. We believed that government was not inherently evil. It could—and should—be an instrument for human progress. Government could be harnessed by the people to create opportunity and justice, and it had a legitimate role as referee in our economy—to keep the playing field level, and to be an active investor in the common good.

I became a social progressive, a military hawk, and a fiscal conservative. I developed a sense of social responsibility (we are our brothers' and sisters' keepers), along with my support for a strong national defense (it really is a dangerous world out there), and a belief that every generation should pay its own way (not borrow from, but invest in our future). During the campaign I attempted to share my life experiences and speak about "finding common ground for the common good."

From Robert Kennedy's 1968 presidential campaign, I shamelessly borrowed "We Can Do Better" as my campaign theme. Of course Bobby said, "We can do betta." Either way, it captured what I wanted to say.

The week in March 2006 when Jon was home for his twenty-fourth birthday, I made three campaign appearances and was preoccupied with preparations for the precinct caucuses on March 7—to be held the day after Jon returned to Utah—the day after I embraced my son for the last time. I spent a great deal of time at my desk writing letters and making phone calls. The Senate District Convention was coming up in April, and I was in competition with another candidate for the party's endorsement. In the hunt for committed delegates, I worked twelve hours a day. Those days were my last opportunity to hang out with Jon.

On Saturday, July 15, 2006, I was out door-knocking, asking for votes. That morning, Jon climbed the Grand Mogul.

After the loss of my son, my life forever changed. The campaign became a faint, background blur. I vaguely remember flying back and forth from climbing and searching for Jon in Idaho, to campaigning in Minnesota, and participating in debates with my opponent.

Megan Boldt, a reporter for the St. Paul *Pioneer Press*, recorded my thoughts in an interview on August 20, 2006:

Francis plans to slowly return to the campaign trail, beginning with a community parade this weekend. He intends to campaign full time after Jon's Sept. 9 memorial service...Francis said he will keep his son's favorite scripture in mind during his campaign: "I've fought the good fight, I have finished the course, I have kept the faith...That was his motto," Francis said, "so I will run the race and keep the faith."

Minneapolis *Star Tribune* columnist Doug Grow also wrote an article about Jon. I'd met Doug in 2005 at an Isaiah Project meeting. The Isaiah Project is a collaboration of church leaders—Roman Catholic, Lutheran, Episcopal, and others—working for social justice.

"Jon was a remarkable young man," I told Doug in August. "I would like people to know more about him." Doug published the article while I was in Idaho, searching with the Mighty Ascension Search Team.

Parents of Missing Rock Climber Aren't Giving Up Yet
—Doug Grow, *Star Tribune*, August 27, 2006

Jon Francis' mail is being routed from his home in Ogden, Utah, to his parents' home in Stillwater. "His Blue Cross bill came," said Jon's father, David. "My wife looked at me—'Should we pay it?'" David knew his spouse, Linda, wasn't really asking a question. She was making a plea: Keep holding onto the hope that Jon might somehow be alive in Idaho's Sawtooth Mountains. "Let's just pay the bill," he said to Linda.

Late in the morning of July 15, Jon Francis reached the summit of Grand Mogul. He signed the register. "All Glory to God for the climb and the beautiful Sawtooths," the 24-year-old man wrote. There's been nothing since. David Francis and Jocelyn, one of his grown daughters, returned to the mountain Thursday, this time with 20 people and specially trained dogs. "This is about body recovery, not a search,"' he said before departing.

Searching's a focused action. Everything else is done in an awful fog. Once in a while, Francis tries to step out of that fog. He's the DFL candidate for the state Senate.

But in these awful days, he said, he won't start pushing hard in his campaign until after a celebration of Jon's life is held Sept. 9 at Ascension Episcopal Church in Stillwater.

For now, Francis wants to talk about his son.

Jon Francis, a young man filled with joy. A Bible camp counselor. A youth director at a church in Ogden. A wonderful athlete. Humble.

"When he was in high school, his [Stillwater High] cross country team won the State championship and they were voted national champions," his father recalled. "Jostens created a special ring for the team, but he wouldn't buy it. I kept telling him, 'You should get one of those. You earned it. It would be something you'll always be proud of.' He told me, 'I don't need a ring. I'll carry what we did in my heart. That's enough.' He always walked humbly with God."

On election night in November, we organized a victory party that was well attended by hopeful friends and supporters. My cousins, Jan and Charlie Brown (yes, Charlie Brown), who had driven from Michigan in September for Jon's memorial service, returned to Minnesota to be with me that night. The Austins, our friends from church, kept track of the vote count on the Internet. I took an early lead in the returns but slipped behind as the northern, more conservative precincts began reporting. By ten p.m., it was clear I lost.

I struggled to make a brief announcement and express thanks to my supporters. We packed up our bunting, flags, pictures, and balloons, and went home. The final result showed that as a part-time, grief-stricken candidate, I had lost by only two-thousand votes (five percent) in a district that is shamelessly gerrymandered to be a safe, conservative stronghold.

I slept fitfully that night, lonely for my son, and questioning why I put myself and my family through the agony of a political campaign.

Chapter 15

THE LONG, CRUEL WINTER

*"In the bleak mid-winter, frosty wind made moan,
earth stood hard as iron, water like a stone;
snow had fallen, snow on snow, snow on snow,
in the bleak mid-winter, long ago."*

—A CHRISTMAS CAROL

In the arcane realm of search and rescue, our summer and fall search efforts were impressive by any standards and the hunt for Jon attracted national attention from the search and rescue community. However, we had failed to find Jon and bring him home. Winter had driven us off the mountain. To add to our gloom, the coming of winter in Minnesota brought dread with the prospect of bleak, cloudy, short, and often bitterly cold days. I more than dreaded that winter; I wasn't sure I could survive it. Jon's loss changed everything. My life was now divided. Life before July 15, 2006, was whole and promising; life after Jon disappeared was hopeless and empty. Jon's body remained somewhere on the Grand Mogul unprotected from the brutal winter elements and hungry predators. No parent, family, or human being should *ever* have to endure these imaginings.

We could not return to the mountain until mid-June at the earliest. Even that goal was optimistic, and totally dependent on the severe, unpredictable Idaho climate. Linda and I held onto each other tightly for months as we weathered the emotional storms, the days of despair, and evenings of tears.

We had changed Jon's address from Joanna's house in Utah to ours in Minnesota. My heart ached every time I received a letter addressed to Jonathan Francis. The most gut-wrenching was his letter of acceptance to Luther Theological Seminary in St. Paul, another stabbing reminder that Jon's promise, his life of ministry and service, would never be fulfilled. Most were dunning letters from creditors. Linda and I tried to talk to the creditors, but we had no standing and no death certificate to resolve his estate. We sought legal advice and were informed that we could petition the court to become conservators. The petition would cost about twenty-five hundred dollars to process, and we would be required to file an annual report with the court thereafter. We decided the best action was to take no action.

Eventually Jon's debts were sent to collection agencies, and the collection calls began. The dialogue became predictable:

"Is Jonathan Francis there?"

"No. This is his father. Can I help you?"

"No, this is a personal matter for Jonathan."

"I'm sorry. My son died in a mountain climbing accident in July."

"I see. Goodbye."

Linda and I sent letters with copies of the missing person flyer to Jon's creditors. It did little good. The process of collection letters and phone calls ground on unabated.

In November, Jon's Augustana College running coach Tracy Hellman ran the Seattle Marathon in his memory. Tracy wore the number Jon planned to wear, and ran the race in tribute to him. He finished in less than three hours—Jon's goal. Mick Garry, sports writer for the

Sioux Falls Argus Leader, heard about Tracy's tribute to Jon, and wrote an inspiring story that quoted Tracy: "Jon was such a positive instrument for Augustana's program," Hellman said. "He brought an energy to everything he did. He was a talented runner, but it was his positive outlook that was most memorable. He was the glue that held the team together."

We began to face all the special days without Jon: our first Thanksgiving without Jon, our first Christmas without Jon.

Christmas used to be my favorite time of year—a season of magic when the world was lit up and decorated for weeks. Beginning in the November after Jon disappeared, I was struck head on with the Christmas theme: the long-awaited gift from God—the birth of His son. Now I was a father who lost his son. Holiday joy became holiday sorrow. However, we followed many of the family Christmas rituals that were important to Jon, rituals that gave our family a sense of connectedness. Linda and I went to the Silver Creek Tree Farm, where we had gone with Jon and our daughters for many years. This year, after we cut down our tree and carried it out of the woods, we tied it to the top of Jon's car. We decorated the tree, tenderly hanging some of Jon's cherished ornaments. We played Barbara Streisand's Christmas album—a favorite of mine and Jon's.

After the holidays mercifully ended, Linda and I decided it was too emotionally difficult to keep Jon's car. We couldn't own it or legally sell it, so we stopped payments, knowing that it would eventually be repossessed. But that meant that we would have to suffer through the predictable—and painful—collection process. Finally after three months of this, I received a phone call from a local towing company requesting a pick-up time and location. Linda said she could not bear to see them tow it from our driveway. So I arranged for the car to be picked up at our mechanic's garage. I drove it to Rick's 36 and left the keys with Pete.

In January 2007 I was finally able to open and read the files on Jon's laptop. I found a gold mine of Jon's papers on religion, his personal letters, poems, and deep thoughts. His writings reflected the life of a remarkable young man who questioned and struggled, but eventually gave his life over to God, celebrated God's creation, and committed himself to serve others with love and joy.

Empowered with the evidence of Jon's profound dedication to helping others, I turned with confidence to the idea of starting a foundation in honor of Jon, to be dedicated to making a positive difference in people's lives, as Jon had, and to pass on Jon's legacy of love and service.

Further, Linda and I decided that we wanted to learn more about search and rescue so we could be more involved and helpful in the coming spring search. We were directed to the National Association for Search and Rescue (NASAR). I logged on to their website and read their mission statement:

> The National Association for Search and Rescue, Inc., (NASAR) is a not-for-profit membership association dedicated to advancing professional, literary, and scientific knowledge in fields related to search and rescue. NASAR is comprised of thousands of paid and non-paid professionals interested in all aspects of search and rescue—the humanitarian cause of saving lives—throughout the United States and around the world...that others may live.

NASAR sponsors training and certification for search and rescue. I signed us up, and Linda and I stayed in La Crosse, Wisconsin, for two weekends of training in March. The instructors from the Nicolet Search Team in Wisconsin were knowledgeable and compassionate. They spent many hours with us, in and out of class, helping us cope with the knowledge, challenge, and grief of a search for a lost loved one.

In class it was impossible not to relate the lessons to what happened during the official search. Reading the chapter on search strategy was the most painful—when we learned about the importance of centering the search on the LKP (last known position). That did not happen in the search for Jon.

By this time, it was warm enough for us to be outside for our land navigation training. Linda and I passed our tests. We achieved SARTECH III. I passed the SARTECH II written exam, but skipped the weekend field test in the Wisconsin wilderness. The instructor agreed that I'd had enough outdoor field experience.

After SAR training, I took up indoor wall climbing because it's good climbing training and core muscle building. Jon had used an indoor climbing wall in Stillwater with his high school coaches, Scott Christensen and David Brandt. I called David and asked if I could climb with them. I wore Jon's climbing harness and we climbed one night a week for several weeks.

At the same time, Linda was reading *Ambiguous Loss* by Pauline Boss, a family therapist. She showed the book to me and said, "Here is the name for our pain." It's a book about people "learning to live with unresolved grief."

That winter, the entire Francis family worked together to create the Jon Francis Foundation (JFF) to "honor Jon's life and to mold our sorrow into hope and purpose." The Jon Francis Foundation would help others coping with unresolved grief and loss. We wanted JFF to provide hope, knowledge, and resources to others who suffered the misfortune of losing a loved one in the wilderness and being abandoned by law enforcement. Also, our intention was to raise public awareness and address deficiencies in SAR capabilities, preparedness, and the lack of equitable funding.

This approach is similar to the efforts of the Jacob Wetterling Foundation, which worked diligently to create the Amber Alert System;

and John Walsh, father of Adam Walsh, who labored long and hard to convince the U.S. Department of Justice to create the National Center for Missing and Exploited Children.

I could not help but think of the old cliché: "Rather than curse the darkness, light a candle." The Francis family decided to light a candle.

Chapter 16

UPON A FOUNDATION

When it comes to finding missing and lost persons, the public sector often lets us down. Our fellow human beings go missing more frequently than most people realize, and law enforcement is often not effective in finding the missing. According to an FBI audit report, in 2006, the year Jon went missing, there were eight hundred unsolved "missing persons" cases in Minnesota, and two hundred unsolved "unidentified remains" cases.

The flawed official search and rescue process causes deep pain and suffering to the loved ones of those missing people. The survivors are victims of unresolved loss. When law enforcement stops their search without finding the lost person, the family is plunged into deep despair—with feelings of abandonment, helplessness, and hopelessness. Not knowing what happened, and not being able to lay your loved one to rest, piles grief upon grief.

In addition, local law enforcement, responsible for search and rescue (SAR), is often inadequately trained, prepared, equipped, and funded. Worst of all (perhaps due to ignorance of the problem), U.S. citizens tolerate gross inequity and unfairness in standards of conduct and funding. For example; the *New York Times* on October 2, 2008, reported that the State of Nevada spent over $600,000 in their months-long search for millionaire Steve Fossett. Based on our search cost experience, Custer County, Idaho, spent about ten thousand dollars and twenty-nine hours searching for Jon Francis.

Before this experience, I never wondered or knew who was responsible for finding those who go missing in the wilderness. The lost and missing are not just out of sight; they are out of our collective awareness. Lost adults are not often topics of political debates. What my family learned in a painful way is that finding missing persons is largely a local issue. I questioned why the responsibility for search and rescue is carried by local sheriffs who may not have the resources and training necessary to handle these types of time-sensitive emergencies. Some states have proposed billing families for the cost of their lost person searches. To the families involved, this is tantamount to being personally charged for having the fire department rescue your house and family from flames.

The current procedures are ineffective and unfair to grieving loved ones, law enforcement, the search and rescue community, and certainly for all the people who pay taxes, elect public servants, and rely on their services. According to *Accidents in North American Mountaineering*, a book published annually by the American Alpine Club that describes numerous mountain climbing accidents and rescues, the most effective rescues are conducted within national parks and the least successful are conducted by inadequately trained and funded county sheriffs. The evidence is clear. Why isn't "search and rescue" a state and national priority with standards of performance and sufficient and equitable funding and resources? Some responsibilities are best carried by national agencies. We don't rely on fifty state militias for our national defense. Why do we place our trust in county sheriffs to find our missing loved ones?

"Upon a foundation, hope"
—Mark Brouwer, *Stillwater Courier,* Wednesday, April 18, 2007

When David Francis lost his son Jon to an Idaho mountain last July, he didn't know much about search and rescue operations. Now he knows more than he could ever have wanted.

Over three dizzying days, the father of four learned that Jon had gone missing during a climb near the church camp where he worked, had rushed with his family to join an official search, and then watched as that search was called off by authorities just as it seemed to be finding its feet.

In the weeks and months that followed, the Francis family exhausted its bodies and their finances in repeated, private searches of the mountain, which gave them clues but no resolution to their ordeal.

Rather than let their bitterly earned expertise go to waste, however, the family has started a foundation so that others who lose loved ones in the wilderness have more resources, direction and hope at their ready.

The family began work on The Jon Francis Foundation after a conversation David Francis had this winter with Nancy Sabin, executive director of the Jacob Wetterling Foundation, which had assisted the Francis family by providing a lost person expert last summer. That foundation (created in the aftermath of the 1989 disappearance of St. Joseph boy Jacob Wetterling) was instrumental in the search. Sabin suggested that the Francis family "consider finding a way to bring some good out of their loss."

Nancy Sabin, executive director of the Jacob Wetterling Resource Center, provided advice in the formation of JFF. She introduced us to the Minnesota Council of Nonprofits, where I took a course, How to Start a Nonprofit. I filled out forms for the Minnesota Secretary of State and the Internal Revenue Service, applying for nonprofit incorporation and tax exempt 501 (C) (3) status. I wrote Jon Francis Foundation articles of incorporation and bylaws, and recruited a founding board of directors. The legal requirements called for two foundation officers: a president and a treasurer. I took the position of president and Linda accepted the treasurer role. Our daughter Jocelyn was named executive director.

I reached out to several friends and colleagues I trusted and admired to create a board to guide us through this maze. I sought out those with entrepreneurial experience, business sense, compassion, and a commitment to making a difference in the world. Above all, I valued integrity. I needed people who would not be afraid say "no" to us when we went off course. We were blessed with an outstanding group of directors who agreed to serve.

We received a wonderful gift from Ian Duvall, a talented artist and a camp counselor with Jon at Luther Heights. Ian had used Jon's image from a photo. The oil painting, a colorful tribute to Jon, shown driving a church youth van in Utah, was printed on postcards and became the visible symbol of the Jon Francis Foundation.

Jocelyn created a design for the Foundation letterhead. At the bottom, I placed a sentence from a Franciscan blessing:

"May God bless you with tears...
to shed for those who suffer
from pain...

so that you may reach out
your hand to comfort them."

The mission of the Jon Francis Foundation (JFF) is to support and empower others coping with the disappearance of a loved one, by providing hope, knowledge, and resources; and to reduce incidents of loss through wilderness safety, training, and information. www.jonfrancis.org

Chapter 17

A SPRING OF HOPE

*"He gives power to the faint, and strengthens the powerless.
Even youths will faint and be weary, and the young will
fall exhausted;*

*but those who wait for the LORD shall renew their
strength, they shall mount up with wings like eagles,
they shall run and not be weary, they shall walk and
not faint."*

ISAIAH 40:29–31 (NRSV)

Like a good omen, the spring of 2007 came early and felt warmer. The
favorable weather added to our sense of hope that we would soon be in
Idaho on the Grand Mogul and at last be able to bring Jon home. I was
haunted by the vision that after nearly a year, our son's once-handsome
face and strong body were now skeletal remains. I desperately wanted
to find Jon before there was nothing left. But I didn't want to be the
one to find him.

The torment of waiting was briefly relieved by several meaningful
events.

MARCH 2007, OGDEN, UTAH

Jocelyn suggested that we hold the Foundation kickoff at Ascension Lutheran in Ogden, Utah, on March 5 to observe Jon's twenty-fifth birthday. Instead of sitting at home, wallowing in sadness on Jon's birthday, we could spend it with the Mighty Ascension Search Team and the many people in Utah who knew and loved Jon. Jocelyn started making the arrangements. We also planned to ski at Snow Basin on Jon's birthday. He often said how much he enjoyed the western powder snow at Snow Basin.

The same incredible people who courageously searched the Grand Mogul for months helped us plan the Jon Francis Foundation Kickoff. We arrived in Ogden on March 1 and met with Joanna Wolf and Cecilia West. Joanna had created a slide show about Jon, our fledgling foundation mission statement, and our vision. For the first time, we met Pastor Renee Kiel, David's wife and co-pastor at Ascension. Pastor Renee had recently returned from Afghanistan where she had served (after recall to active duty) as an Army chaplain.

Jocelyn, Doug, Audrey, and Charlie Plass—or the "Plasstastics," as Jocelyn called her family—joined us. We shopped at Walmart for decorations, feeling pangs of guilt because we remembered how much Jon disliked that chain, but it was convenient. We bought green table runners, the color of the Jon Francis Foundation, and bought small rocks for guests to take home to remember the evening.

The Mighty Ascension Search Team was there, many members of the church, and representatives from the Huntsville Public Library where Jon had worked part-time. I managed to say a few words about the Foundation. Joanna's slide show was superb, starting with pictures of Jon from his birth and culminating with his mountaintop picture taken on Thomason peak in the Sawtooths. The show was also the public debut of the Jon Francis Foundation postcard (Ian's tribute to his friend) that Jocelyn commissioned.

For me, the evening is a blur, though the event was well attended—a successful kickoff and fundraiser. Pastor Renee had to remind me to introduce the other (non-Ascension) guests from the library. The loving people at Ascension put together a wonderful banquet.

On Sunday, we worshipped with our friends at "Ascension West" (as we began to call the church). Linda and I met with the youth again. They showed signs of healing. We gave each of them a rock to hold onto to remind them of Jon.

After enduring too many special days at home alone, I was relieved to be in Utah for Jon's birthday on Monday. Jeff Turner donated lift tickets to Snow Basin. Linda and I, Joanna Wolf, and the Plasstastics enjoyed a beautiful, sunny day on the same slopes that Jon loved so much. Three-year-old Audrey went on the bunny hill.

That evening, we held a thank-you dinner for our hosts at a downtown Ogden restaurant. Jon's birthday dinner felt like a family reunion. On the flight back to Minnesota, Linda and I agreed that it had been a good decision to go to Utah in March and to be immersed in one of Jon's most loving communities of faith.

April 2007, Stillwater, Minnesota

Every spring for over forty years, during Stillwater Area High School's track season, the school hosted an invitational track meet called the Pony Classic. Jon ran in four Pony Classics. Scott Christensen called me to let me know that on Saturday, April 21, 2007, he was dedicating the 3200 meter race to Jon and it would hereafter be named the Jon Francis 3200 Meter Team Race. Scott invited us to be present and to give out the awards.

On a chilly Saturday morning, we arrived at the Stillwater High School track. I'd been given an incorrect time, so we missed the race. Linda and I felt a sting of disappointment. We sat in the stands with Tom and Mary Swanson. The Swanson and Francis families had traveled many miles together for many years to watch our son Jon and their son Andy run as teammates in high school, and as competitors in college. We talked about the meets and the memories. I recalled how Jon was frustrated and envious that Andy got ready for the season in only two weeks, and emerged in competitive condition. Jon trained all year long.

Linda and I had attended Andy's wedding. We recalled fondly how Jon and Andy and the others danced with abandon as if it were senior prom night.

Fortunately, we hadn't missed the award ceremony. Scott had ensured that his best four were in the race to win it for Jon, and I had the pleasure of presenting the first place trophies in the Jon Francis 3200 Meter Team Race to the Stillwater team.

Jon was further recognized in the *Stillwater Gazette*, our hometown newspaper. His coach paid tribute to Jon by saying, "One of the things with naming an athletic event after somebody is that you don't dwell on the sorrow or the mournful part of it; you rejoice. Jon was the top two-miler in the Pony Classic twice, and he did it by running from the front."

MAY 2007, OGDEN, UTAH

Jon's faith community in Ogden, "Ascension West," planned to dedicate their annual 5K Grace Race to Jon in May. Jon helped organize the 2006 event, came in first, and established a course record. I was invited to participate, and I assured the organizers that I would not be the first to finish. They created a race shirt with Jon's picture on it. I flew out to Ogden and helped stuff bags with race giveaways, information about the Jon Francis Foundation, and Sport Beans donated by Jocelyn's friend Janice from the Jelly Belly Company.

Expecting warmer weather, I failed to pack enough layers to wear during the race. The temperature was 32 degrees Fahrenheit at the start, and I struggled to warm up in my shorts and short-sleeve Jon Francis shirt. I thought about all of the races Jon ran in Minnesota winters, wearing only a light shirt and his running shorts. I finished, but was unable to win in my age group.

Fortunately, there was no snow on the ground in Ogden that May, so I made my first trip to the Ogden Botanical Garden to see the tree planted by his friends from the Huntsville Public Library. Jon had worked part-time at the library, located in a beautiful area near Snow Basin.

The previous fall, the grieving staff in Huntsville had planted a Burr oak tree in remembrance of Jon. I sat by the Jonathan tree for an hour, wept, and spoke with my son.

"Jon, I miss you."

Dad, I'm fine...Dad, you've never been a sad person; don't be sad now.

"Easy for you to say, Jon...Jon, I love you."

I love you, Dad.

When I returned from Utah, Linda was completing work on her JFF Safety Kit. She was inspired to do something tangible, simple, and practical that would make a difference. Linda often cited stories about hunters who became injured or lost in the wilderness and did not have a reliable signaling method to attract the attention of nearby searchers. The kit contained wilderness safety and survival tips, a loud whistle, and a mirror. These low-cost, low-technology signaling devices would be valuable to a lost person.

Linda and I, with the help of many from "Ascension East" in Stillwater, planned our first Minnesota informational meeting and fundraiser to support the foundation and help finance the spring search. This was the last JFF event before we headed for Idaho. Jeff Hasse agreed to present his "Jon Francis Case Study."

For the national search and rescue community, Jeff had prepared a PowerPoint presentation with documentation on the long, complex search for Jon. This was the first time that members of Ascension Episcopal (our church), Jon Francis Foundation directors, and the community saw the rugged, treacherous terrain we were covering. Many expressed shock at their first sight of the massive mountain.

When Mary Divine, whom I first met on the campaign trail, returned from maternity leave, she became my main contact with the *Pioneer Press*. She had tears in her eyes during our interviews. An excellent writer, she captured the distress we were feeling. Mary interviewed me about the Jon Francis Foundation, Jon's twenty-fifth birthday, and the plan for our spring search.

"Searching for Jon"

—Mary Divine, *Pioneer Press*, March 4, 2007

With their 24-year-old son still missing on an Idaho mountain, David and Linda Francis of Stillwater are working to help others, even as they struggle to reconcile themselves to his fate. But this summer, the family will resume their search and, they hope, bring Jon home.

Jeff and I finally completed the planning and preparation for the 2007 search for Jon. He wrote an excellent incident action plan to guide our search. We were full of hope and confidence that all we had learned and all that we had accomplished in 2006 would lead us to Jon. However, the search start date was a problem. I was pushing for a June 15 start. But if the snow and ice on the Grand Mogul did not recede by then, the spring search team would be sitting in winter camp waiting for the thaw. This would be a devastating, expensive mistake. I often thought of General Eisenhower in World War II, agonizing over the start date for D-Day.

I sought information and advice from Erik Leidecker of the Sawtooth Mountain Guides. Erik reported that the Sawtooths had lower than average snow depth during that winter, and was experiencing an early spring thaw. He pointed me to a website that reported snow depths on several peaks in Idaho. The closest reporting station to the Grand Mogul was Vienna Mines. Every morning that spring, Linda looked on the Internet at the live Stanley, Idaho, web camera shot of the mountains and surrounding cattle lands. I studied the receding snow depth at Vienna Mines.

Jeff allowed me to make the decision. I called a June 15 start and gained commitments. Linda arranged flights for our searchers, handlers, and search dogs. Jocelyn found and rented a house for us in Sawtooth City. We planned to stay in Idaho until we found Jon. I sent a letter to the Custer County sheriff to inform him that we were returning to Idaho in June, and that we would request his help in carrying Jon's remains off the mountain.

Chapter 18

ON THE SUMMIT

MAY 2007, SAWTOOTH CITY, IDAHO

On the way to Idaho, Linda and I encountered snow-covered mountain roads in Montana. After three days of driving, we arrived in Sawtooth City. We moved into our rented house on Smiley Creek, where we had a panoramic view of the Sawtooth Mountains that had attracted our son like a siren. Doug had dropped out of the PhD program at the University of California, Davis, to return with Jocelyn to Idaho.

I met our new landlady, Marlies Stroes. Marlies was born in Germany. Her husband, Guus, was born in Holland, and they now lived year-round in Idaho. Marlies, outspoken, assertive, and compassionate, quickly expressed her sympathy and her desire to take part in the search. She and her search dog China (pronounced Cheena) were training to be members of Custer County Search and Rescue. We talked often about climbing and SAR tactics. She loaned me her copy of the National Geographic Topographic maps of the Sawtooth Range, which I downloaded onto my computer.

We set up our new command center. Linda and Jocelyn had ordered house phones, cell phones, and Internet service. We had two laptops and a desktop computer. We still had bitter memories of our months in communications hell the year before and we were determined not to suffer that fate again.

The boat we purchased in Boise arrived and we named it *Searching for Jon*. The well-worn, faded yellow, seventeen-foot fiberglass Bayliner had a 115 HP Mercury outboard. Having our own boat gave us more flexibility and reduced the expense of shuttle fees across Redfish Lake.

I settled in, made phone calls, and sent emails to batten down the logistics and resources for our Friday, June 15 climb. Our plan was to climb to the tarn at 8,500 feet, set up a base camp, and search up from there. Resting the people and dogs at a high camp would give us more time and energy to search high on the summit block. That's where Jon was—somewhere on the summit block, on the rock above the tree line.

Linda and I met with Ed Cannady of the Forest Service. Ed, a tall, strong, and gracious gentleman, briefed us on SNRA campsite rules and gave us a firsthand account of his search efforts for Jon the previous year. Ed had combed some of the more difficult terrain near the summit. He was comfortable with our plan, knowing that the Sawtooth Mountain Guides (SMG) were in charge of the high camp and were trained in "Leave no trace"—leaving our campsite unspoiled and cleaner than we found it.

Erik Leidecker described the preparations and services that SMG would provide. Next, to see for myself, I hiked five miles on the eastern Redfish Lake trail and took pictures of the Grand Mogul to see how much of the mountain was still covered in snow. I estimated thirty percent snow coverage above the tree line.

We received over the Internet the aerial photos of the Grand Mogul taken by Calvin Shalk, a member of the Mighty Ascension Search Team. Calvin flew a private plane and carried Larry West and his son, Garret, who took high-resolution pictures of the entire mountain. We examined them to exhaustion, vainly looking for signs of Jon.

Jeff Hasse arrived in Sawtooth City and we reviewed the Incident Action Plan (IAP) that he had prepared for the spring search. The first 2007 Spring Search Team had arrived and we assembled at the Redfish Lake Lodge docks where Jon had boarded the shuttle on the morning of July 15, 2006, and where we had departed countless times over four months for the five-mile ride across Redfish Lake to the Grand Mogul. This time, we were transporting people in our *Searching for Jon* boat.

The team spent the evening of June 14 at the Redfish Lake Inlet Camp. I sat at the campfire that night, filled with hope and purpose. The next morning, we started the long climb to the tarn. The tarn is a small mountain lake at 8,500 feet on the east side of the Grand Mogul. Early in the year it remains a good source of water before it gets overgrown with what Erik called "red crawly things" (small red crustaceans) in July. The climb is several miles and 2,000 vertical feet from Redfish Lake. We hiked the forest service trail up to 8,000 feet, and traversed down the steep ridge into the forest drainage area. We crossed the drainage area, frequently bushwhacking, into a rocky area below the summit. The last 600 feet of the climb was the hardest. A thirty- to forty-degree slope went through forest, scree, and boulders to the final boulder fortress that surrounded the tarn. The east side of the mountain was nearly snow and ice free. I carried a fifty-pound backpack that contained my camping equipment, safety items, first-aid kit, food, and water. I felt like a Tibetan Sherpa hired to carry a heavy load on a Mount Everest expedition.

This was my highest climb on the Grand Mogul before gaining the summit the next day. We made camp that night with the help of the Sawtooth Mountain Guides who provided tents, food, and water purification. Erik Leidecker was our guide. Our June search objectives were the summit block, the Northeast Ridge, high along the Lopez Route, the toe of Northeast Ridge, the bowl below the Boy Scout Couloir, accessible terrain below the west face, and the lower route to Braxon Peak, a neighboring peak to the northwest.

At high camp were Jeff Hasse and canine teams from three states. The ground teams were made up of experienced mountaineers from across the country. On Saturday, June 16, I prepared to make my first climb to the 9,733 foot summit of the Grand Mogul. I wanted to honor Jon, read his entry in the summit registry, and try to get into his head to figure out which descent route might have looked the most attractive to him. Which way did he decide to go down?

We rose early and had a warm breakfast of oatmeal and coffee. To take advantage of daylight and cool temperatures, we planned to start our search and climb by seven a.m. I put on several layers of clothing. The final layer was my Augustana College windbreaker.

Erik Leidecker led me and my climbing partners, Bart Green and Bill Dooley, up a vast scree field. After many years of running, and months of hiking and climbing, my legs were strong. I was almost fearless on the mountain, capable and confident since Erik taught me to take baby steps and plant my feet firmly in the loose scree that always tried to escape from under my boots and pull me down like quicksand. After several hours of slogging through a thirty- to forty degree slope of scree, we arrived on the summit block.

We worked our way between and around giant boulders—some the size of houses. As we approached within 300 feet of the summit, Erik issued safety helmets and roped us up. On our final assault to the summit, I experienced one moment of concern. Erik pulled me around a large boulder with virtually no foothold. I was exposed. If the rope, harness, or Erik hadn't held, I was in danger of falling hundreds of feet to my death. The four of us worked as a team scrambling, pulling, and sometimes being pulled up by Erik until we finally stood at the summit.

The view was spectacular and breathtaking. At all points on the horizon were mountain peaks: Mount Heyburn and Braxon close by, the White Clouds to the east, the jagged Sawtooths to the west, south, and north. I recognized the Elephant's Perch and Thompson Peak—the highest summit in the Sawtooths—but others I couldn't recognize or name. I felt the mountaintop high, that experience of euphoria and celebration. But the feeling was brief. I was nearly immune to the experience. My mission was to arrive at the summit, not to celebrate.

My mind turned quickly to the business at hand, the reason I made the climb. I opened the rusty, old ammunition box that stored and protected the summit log. Inside was a diary containing handwritten entries going back to 1965. Most signed their names, listed their homes, and gave some information about their ascent routes and experience. Many complained about the difficult climb. The majority expressed their sense of exultation and accomplishment.

I made my entry: "David Francis, June 16, 2007. Stillwater, Minnesota. Father of Jon Francis. Climbed from the tarn to search for and honor my son Jon, missing since July 15, 2006."

In my mind I asked again, *God, where were you? Why didn't you guide Jon's feet off this mountain?*

Next, Erik and I discussed the possible descent routes. Looking down from the summit, we were in agreement that the most attractive and safe descents appeared to be down the east side to the tarn, then proceeding either east into the drainage area, or north through the boulder fields back to the avalanche field.

Because we chose to return the way we went up, we safely descended east to our high camp at the tarn and waited there for the other search parties to return. At our evening debrief, we recorded no new clues other than some dog interest north of our campsite.

June 17, the third and final day of our team's endeavor, yielded no results. So much work and hope had once more ended in failure. We broke camp and made the 2,000-foot descent back to the Redfish Lake Transfer Camp. Jeff and I returned to our Sawtooth City search headquarters house to document the search and finalize the assignments for the next two teams due to arrive.

For fifteen days in June, we scoured a large area of the mountain, including surrounding lakes and forest. Jeff Hasse led Chuck Wooters from Pennsylvania, and his certified cadaver dog, Falco, into the bowl on the north side. Falco showed some interest. Johnny Unser and Taz joined us for their sixth mission. I led Curt and Cathy Orde (from Wyoming) and K-9 Moose along the forest service trail, through the eastern drainage area, and up the steep talus slope on the east side. Our mission was to return to the location of clue number six, the foul odor. We were stopped just short of those GPS coordinates. Moose was unable to maintain his footing in the scree just below the clue location. We were forced to retreat.

Jon's college running coach, Tracy Hellman, searched for three days. I joined Chuck and two others climbing on the west side of the Grand Mogul, slogging through talus until we were stopped by tall granite spires.

Guided by Erik Leidecker, I made my second climb to the summit. This time, Erik took me to the small lake on the north side. As we climbed through the trees, Erik asked me why I doggedly continued the search for Jon.

I thought it was a strange question. I nearly responded with, "If it were your child, wasting away on this mountain, what would you do?" Instead, I explained that it was unnatural and unacceptable to leave Jon's body on a mountain. I couldn't live with that. I was determined to find Jon and bring his remains home for a respectful burial. In addition, we didn't want reports of climbers finding his clothing and body parts for years to come. I took Erik's silence as understanding.

Erik and I climbed over the boulder field and through a notch in the northeast ridge they called "the secret squirrel door." We followed Jon's route through the scree on the northeast ridge to the summit block. At one point, we squeezed through a gulley full of ice and snow. After spending a brief time on the summit, we decided to descend and search Outside Chance to the south. It was a long and tiring descent, stepping and sliding through deteriorated granite that often let loose and flowed around my boots like a river.

By the time we returned to the *Searching for Jon* boat on Redfish Lake, I had been on my feet climbing upward or downward for eleven hours. I was sore and exhausted. When our June effort ended on June 30, we had invested more than fifty search days with no compelling clues and no success. We issued a press release describing our June quest and asked for more volunteers.

I was overcome by waves of hopelessness and waning confidence that we would ever find Jon's body and bring him off that cruel mountain. I talked with Jeff and many of the searchers about our lack of success. "Where is my son?" I pleaded.

Jeff analyzed our results and created an updated plan. Jim Hanley, one of our most faithful and optimistic searchers, encouraged me for the umpteenth time to contact Andy Rebman of K-9 Specialty Search Associates in Kent, Washington, and author of *Cadaver Training Handbook*. Andy is a retired Connecticut State Trooper and canine handler who has participated in over a thousand searches since 1972. He is internationally recognized as a leader in this field.

I called Andy and asked if he would evaluate our clues, and give me some advice. He agreed, and called me back a few days later. Andy asked me one simple question: "Where have the majority of accidents and rescues taken place on the Grand Mogul?"

The answer was—the north face.

In addition to a group of Boy Scouts who had once been cliffed out there and needed to be rescued, shortly before Jon vanished, a group of employees of the Redfish Lake Lodge were stranded and endangered on the north side of the Grand Mogul. After having been given bad information that it was the best route to use, they had attempted to ascend the north face. I passed this on to Jeff. His analysis of the past results led him to that conclusion as well. We agreed that the July search would concentrate on the difficult north side of the mountain.

In August 2006, the upper 600 feet of the north side summit block had been rappelled and searched by three members of the Mighty Ascension Search Team. However, since then, most of our search efforts and resources were spent on the east side. I contributed to this choice because for months I insisted that Jon would have descended the same way he went up. That's what some of Jon's climbing partners believed. Now it was apparent where we had to go next. Even our friend Annie, who possesses psychic abilities, was directing us into an area on the north side. We knew we needed to go back into the riskiest and most treacherous terrain on the Grand Mogul—the north face. We knew that it was our last, best hope of finding Jon.

Chapter 19

REMAINS

"If we keep demanding that God will yield up His answers, perhaps someday we will understand them. And then we shall be something more than clever apes, and we shall dance with God. I cannot defeat God in an argument; I avoid the idea... I return today. I will walk the middle path. There is a time to question and a time of assurance. I will walk the questioning path and I will walk the listening, praying and receiving paths as well."

—JON FRANCIS

When I first held my son Jonathan minutes after his birth on Friday, March 5, 1982, I was filled with joy and hope for his future. Twenty-five years later, my remaining hope was that I could retrieve most of his body and lay him to rest with dignity.

July 15, 2007, marked the first anniversary of the loss of our son. We were living in a rental house in Sawtooth City, Idaho, deciding on the next phase in our recovery effort. Jocelyn, Doug, and a number of others grieving Jon's death were planning to gain the summit of the Grand Mogul, guided by Erik Leidecker, to honor Jon and to cope with the anguish brought on by the first anniversary. Mike Goodwin, Jon's best friend and running partner from Augustana, and his wife Megan had come to Idaho.

While Jocelyn, Doug, and Mike were on the mountain, Linda, Megan, and I took our grandchildren to Sandy Beach on Redfish Lake for the day. Katie, our eleven-year-old granddaughter from Minnesota, had flown out and was staying with us the week before she was attending camp at Luther Heights. Sitting at a picnic table in view of the Grand Mogul, a butterfly landed on Katie. Linda extended her hand, held it close, and the butterfly moved to her finger. It lingered for several minutes on Linda's finger, then flew away. We had never experienced such close contact with a butterfly. In tears, we were convinced that it was a sign from our son assuring us of his love and peace. Jocelyn, Doug, and Mike returned late to Sawtooth City, exhausted and excited. We told them about the butterfly, and they told us about the climb and their view from the summit.

Jeff Hasse had created the July recovery objectives, and maps of the north face. The deteriorating rock terrain on the north face is steep, slippery, and treacherous. Much of the north face, including the Chockstone Couloir, was covered with snow and ice that summer.

Jeff carefully considered which experienced, technical mountain-climbing teams to recruit. I encouraged him to give the assignment to the best we'd worked with, the Sawtooth Mountain Guides. "Okay. It's your call," Jeff said.

I contacted Erik Leidecker and asked him if he was willing and able to assemble a team to assault the north face. He accepted, but advised me that some of the guides were feeling serious emotional fatigue after nearly a year of climbing and searching.

They, after all, were employees of SMG because they valued being mountain guides. Searching for remains was not their primary occupation. But the guides had become emotionally committed to helping us find our son.

On Monday, July 23, the guides climbed to the bowl on the north face below the summit and set up camp. They roped up and began climbing, rappelling, and searching the gullies on the north that were designated by letters on our search plan. They returned to camp that night. The next morning, Tuesday, July 24, they made several long and difficult repels on the west side of the Chockstone Couloir to investigate possible exit routes. But they found nothing. On the way back to camp, Drew Daly, a summer intern with SMG, was attracted by a bright object in a snow pack. They went over to look, and spotted a buckle from a hiker's backpack. Nearby they saw Jon's remains.

The guides called Erik, who phoned to tell me that our son had been found. I experienced a few seconds of elation, a few breaths of closure. Then grief poured in. Never again would there be any doubt, uncertainty, or faint hope that our son was alive. We now had the physical remains, the evidence of our son's death.

As required and arranged, Erik called Custer County Sheriff Tim Eiken and requested an official party to investigate the crime scene and carry Jon's remains off the mountain. We knew that the site of the accident would be treated as a possible crime scene—in the event of foul play—and that it had to be investigated by law enforcement.

We called our daughters Robin and Melissa with the stark news, and I phoned Jeff Hasse in Minnesota. Jeff said he would be on the next flight to Boise. To celebrate their eighth wedding anniversary, Jocelyn and Doug had taken their kids camping on a remote lake. We had no way to reach them. Cory at the Smiley Creek Café offered to go to Yellow Belly Lake to track them down. He found their campsite but it was too late for them to safely break camp and canoe out until the next morning.

Due to the lateness the crime scene investigation and the transport of Jon off the mountain also had to wait until morning. The Sawtooth Mountain Guides marked the location with a cairn, a Scottish word that means a collection of rocks to mark a trail, or create a landmark or a monument. They established a vigil and camped nearby overnight on the mountain. Meanwhile, Custer County was assembling an incident command center once again at Sandy Beach.

That evening, Linda and I drove out to Sandy Beach to meet with the sheriff's deputies. Levi, the new incident commander, introduced himself and advised me that he was in charge, and that all communications needed to go through him. Deputy Luanna Gunderson, the compassionate, straightforward, tobacco-chewing driver of the Custer County sheriff's rescue boat, was present again.

The plan was to send the official investigation and remains recovery team on the mountain the next morning, Wednesday, July 25. They were to meet with the Sawtooth Mountain Guides who were holding a respectful vigil at the crime scene. Together, they would transport Jon's remains on the sheriff's boat back across Redfish Lake.

I briefly considered climbing to the place where Jon was found. After months of mountain climbing, I was fit and capable enough to make the ascent. Erik had given me the coordinates:

44 degrees. 05.010′ N
114 degrees. 57.058′ W
Elevation 8248′

By now, I could plug them into my GPS and lay out a track. I didn't, because it would have meant leaving Linda alone. Jocelyn and her family had not yet arrived from their camping trip. Finally, I chose to accept the gift freely offered by so many generous people. My final memory of Jon would be his handsome smile, his strong body, and his warm touch on his twenty-fourth birthday, not the sight of his skeletal remains scattered in a rock pile.

WEDNESDAY, JULY 25, SANDY BEACH ON REDFISH LAKE

Early in the morning Linda and I traveled to Sandy Beach once again to meet Sheriff Eikens. He was friendly and consoling. Vicki Armbruster, the Custer County coroner, was attentive and sensitive as well. The parking lot containing an enclosure and several police vehicles was roped off with police tape. Levi, the incident commander, was busy on his radio, communicating with the authorities on the mountain. Vicki spoke softly with us about Jon and about any arrangements we might have made for the disposition of his body.

To make a positive identification, Linda gave Vicki Jon's dental records, which she had been carrying for months. But we had no doubt that it was Jon. No one else had been reported missing on the Grand Mogul. We asked Vicki to collect, retain, and inventory Jon's remains and personal effects. She informed us that she was not able to store Jon's remains, and that we would need to hire a local funeral director. I called our funeral director, Nicki, at Simonet's Funeral Home in Stillwater and asked her to locate an Idaho funeral director to help us. Only one mortician was listed in Custer County. He was hired.

Tim Eikens assured us that they would do everything they could to find everything they could. As we waited for the police boat to return, I envisioned the solemn honor guard, which Jeff had directed in his incident action plan to carry Jon's body back to us. But that did not happen. Abruptly, the police boat, mounted on its trailer, sped away carrying our son's remains in several plastic bags. I asked Levi where the remains would be kept. He said they would be held temporarily at the sheriff's office in Stanley. He planned to hold a "debrief" at the City Hall at six p.m., and we were "welcome" to attend.

That evening, we gathered at the Stanley City Hall. Jocelyn and Doug met us there. We sat in a large circle of folding chairs. The sheriff started the meeting by thanking everyone for their work. I expressed my family's appreciation and asked that the effort continue to find "as much of Jon" as we could and to continue looking for his personal effects. Jon's black-and-yellow day pack, with most of its contents, was still somewhere on the mountain.

The meeting concluded with the sheriff directing Erik and SMG to search the high, steep technical areas, and for his deputy to put a team together to search the bowl. Jeff Hasse arrived from Minnesota just before the meeting adjourned. He offered to meet with the coroner and jointly examine Jon's remains. Jeff, Linda, Jocelyn, Doug, and I drove to the sheriff's office in Stanley and met with the coroner, along with Deputy Talbot, and the Idaho mortician hired by our Minnesota funeral home.

The mortician was gregarious, ebullient, and unfocused. Expecting a dour and comforting presence, I was uneasy with the encounter. However, we went ahead and authorized the transfer. Several times, I repeated our family's wishes. Since the authorities would not retain Jon's remains, we voiced our expectation that the Idaho mortician provide safekeeping until we completed the recovery. When the long search was finally over, we wanted to bring Jon home to be buried in the place where he was born and baptized.

Linda and I were again filled with questions. Why did Jon decide to climb the Grand Mogul alone? Why did he choose to descend the north face? What happened? Why did he fall? What decisions and steps led to his death on the Grand Mogul? We wanted to know, but at the same time, we didn't want to know.

I asked the coroner for the cause of Jon's death.

"Massive, blunt force trauma to his head," Vicki said. It appeared that Jon had fallen a great distance, and that his death was immediate.

That was an important answer to one of the many questions that had haunted us: Did Jon suffer? We knew Jon had died alone. Now we knew he did not suffer alone. It was strange solace to know that our son died instantly.

Jon's wallet was found in the pocket of his hiking pants inside a sealed plastic bag to keep it dry in the event he fell into water. However, the wallet was now moldy. Jeff volunteered to disinfect and examine the contents. He wore a mask and rubber gloves as he worked outside on the porch. Linda and I were later relieved that we didn't discard the moldy wallet when we learned that Jon's close friend Matt had hand-crafted the wallet as a gift to Jon.

Jeff began work on the accident reconstruction. We learned that most climbing accidents are caused by human error and wrong, unfortunate decisions, and that most accidents happen on the descent when the climber is tired and sometimes in a hurry to "just get back down."

Why did Jon choose to descend the north face? It appeared to be the most direct route from the summit. Jon often chose to descend through gullies. The Chockstone Couloir is a direct and attractive gully. It's composed of slippery scree and a patchy snow, ice, and rock surface that slopes at a forty-degree incline. Because it's technical climbing terrain, too difficult to proceed safely without equipment, climbers were advised to use ropes and harnesses.

Was Jon in a hurry to catch the three p.m. shuttle ride across Redfish Lake? Perhaps he didn't know the Grand Mogul as well as he should have and didn't know how challenging a north face descent would be. If he did, he may have chosen to take the challenge, trusting in his strength and climbing experience.

Jon probably moved down the Couloir with joy and confidence as he had on many of his previous descents. As Jon came face to face with the Chockstone, he must have realized that he could not scramble around it. He needed to turn back and return to the summit or exit the Couloir. The best route to continue down and out of the gully appeared to be along the ledges and cliffs on his left, to the west.

I don't know how Jon felt at the time. Maybe he became concerned for his safety. Was he anxious, or still confident that he had the strength and ability to scramble out? Exiting on the northwestern ridge, he lost his footing and slipped, or tripped, and fell. That's what we think happened.

I asked Erik Leidecker if Jon had shown poor judgment by attempting to scramble down the north face. "No. Many people have safely scrambled the north face," Erik said. "But Jon would have had to make a lot of good decisions."

Jon had done most of his climbing with partners. Those partners told us that he was cautious by nature—not reckless. He had tried to find a partner for his climb of the Grand Mogul on that Saturday. Several people declined, but that did not stop Jon from going out into the wilderness alone. Jon decided to climb solo that day.

Would it have made a difference if Jon had not been alone? That is one of many things we will never know.

NORTH FACE GULLIES

Chapter 20

LEAVING HOME

To Jon Francis, hiking and climbing alone provided a special and unique experience—a spiritual bond between him and nature. That bond with nature was inherent to Jon's life-long faith journey.

As parents, we did our best to give our children roots (a sense of place and home) and wings (the confidence and courage to fly away from the nest). Linda and I gave Jon deep roots as well as strong wings.

Just before he graduated from high school, Jon found a Christian college he was excited about. Augustana is a small Lutheran College located in Sioux Falls, South Dakota. We attended the freshman orientation in the Augustana Chapel with him. The dean of students talked about the importance of diversity and the need to get to know others who were different than you. I looked around the chapel filled with blondes, turned to Jon, and said, "You're the diversity here—the non-blonde, non-Scandinavian, non-Lutheran student!"

At Augustana, Jon worked tirelessly to understand his faith and to live it through his works. He was active in Habitat for Humanity and Campus Crusade for Christ. At the same time, he was a Bible Study leader and a mentor to Hispanic children for Lutheran Social Services and the Sioux Falls School District.

Linda and I wanted Jon to come home during his summer breaks from college to be with us and help around the house. We felt his

"Make connections; let rip..."
by Jon Francis (2004)

I borrowed a quote from Annie Dillard's *Pilgrim at Tinker Creek:*
"Make connections, let rip; and dance where you can."

I let rip with joy when I quietly peruse the contents of the forest floor. I break forth when I shout from a mountain peak after climbing to the top.

My bursting forth takes the form of celebration, of grace, of awe and wonder, of humility and of thanksgiving. I am celebrating the goodness of nature. I am thankful for the goodness of the created world.

I do not know why, but I am closer to God when I am outside. Little Carnelian Lake lies as the crow flies, 500 meters from my front door. The sandy beach, located lakeshore at the end of the township park is half a mile by foot away from my house.

There is trail made of sand, dirt, and gravel that winds its way through the woods to the lakeshore. This trail, the lake, and the park all constitute together my favorite place.

Countless times I have asked, what would I do without that lake and little patch of woods? Between the gravel parking lot and the small sandy beach is my haven and my refuge.

I do not remain silent. I give glory to God for her abundant creation. There is goodness all round. There is goodness deep within.

combination of athletic and academic scholarships and a campus job was enough contribution to his school expenses. But Jon felt that he needed to do more. In 2001, Jon, then nineteen, applied for a summer counselor position with Luther Heights Bible Camp. I found Jon's application letter on his computer.

My qualifications for being a counselor include, being a leader at two Teens Encounter Christ weekends and being involved in three other weekends. In early high school, I volunteered for two weeks at Gethsemane Day Camp in Minneapolis. I have been a delegate and on a youth panel at the annual convention for the Episcopal Church of Minnesota. I was a peer counselor at Stillwater High School as well as a Track and Cross Country captain.

From 1998 to 2000, I taught Sunday school at Ascension Episcopal, and during the summer of 2000, I was a "nanny" for two elementary (school) age boys. Presently, I am a mentor at Edison Middle School in Sioux Falls and helping plan a retreat for college Christians. There are many people who have influenced my faith journey. Primarily there are my parents, who raised me in a Christian home and exposed me to a Christian lifestyle. My parents gave me the tools that have allowed me to enter into Christianity. Another large influence was my youth leader, Rev. LeeAnne Watkins. She sparked my interest and desire to find community and to take further steps toward Christianity.

I became involved in youth group, community service, and youth ministries all because of LeeAnne. She helped shape my young, but unfortunately immature, faith. She was honest, loving, and open to us. She helped me invite myself and put down my roots into a religious life.

A lot of my friends from the Teens Encounter Christ program have made a large impact on my life. My friends Nick, Katrina, Amanda, and Kelsey have all made my life better. I am still friends with all of them, and we converse and meet each other year after year. These four especially taught me how to love excitedly, and how to be a friend.

We are all in separate places right now, but I will never forget how they've cared for me. I turn to these friends still in my times of deep questioning, worry, disappointment, and joy. I trust and love all of them more because we shared a part of God together. These friends still excite and encourage me. I continue in my faith because each of these people has shared a part of their faith, in various forms, with me.

I began some deep questioning of Christianity at the end of my senior year of high school. After a year of mulling over these questions, I found myself in a completely different situation. I didn't have a will, a mind, a faith, or a life that fit together for Christianity anymore. I moved away, pushed away, and held at arm's length skepticism about the life that I had before.

I do not think that I would ever be able to claim a real and significant faith if I had not gone through my period of deep reckoning. Our pastor, Paul Rohde, at Augustana tells me that a questioning faith is seen as more real than a blind following faith. I tend to believe him.

My close friend Alexis helped push along my deep questions and doubts about Christianity. My worldview and mindset were changed by her ideas. Alexis had become a passionate and dedicated Christian. In time she encouraged my journey toward a new formation of faith. Alexis and I discuss our faith life weekly and still share our lives together.

When Jon was a senior at Augustana, he called on the phone to say, "Dad, I've decided to become a Lutheran." Linda and I had seen the process evolving over the years. We knew that raising a child in Minnesota and sending him off to a Lutheran college probably meant an eventual conversion to Lutheranism. Jon was excited about the youth ministry that the ELCA (Evangelical Lutheran Church in America) was doing, and he wanted to be part of it.

"Jon, you'll still be a Christian; won't you?" I teased.

He assured me that he would.

I remained in awe of Jon's ability to maintain a 3.5 grade point average through college, compete in Division II athletics, hold a part-time campus job, and also participate in such a significant ministry in the community. Jon had been on the five-year plan, earning three majors—religion, Spanish, and international studies. Due to his earned scholarships and campus and summer jobs, Jon left college with no student loans. In his fifth year of eligibility, he voluntarily gave up his athletic scholarship, so his coach could use the money to attract fresh talent.

May 22, 2005, Augustana College, Sioux Falls, South Dakota

Jon's sister Melissa and niece Katie traveled with us to his graduation ceremony. Jon was the only graduate to wear "Thanks Mom and Dad" taped on the top of his cap. (He also wore flip-flops and shorts under his gown.) Jon's sense of fun and commitment to diversity added to Augustana's student culture. When we attended a reception at the home of the college president, Dr. Halverson expressed genuine affection and respect for Jon and his contributions to campus life.

During his college semester abroad in Guatemala, Jon had worked at an orphanage, willing to do whatever the job called for, helping the kids or even shoveling pig manure. Jon showed maturity, leadership, and a responsible work ethic in every position he filled—team captain, leader at TEC, camp counselor—even as a dishwasher during high school. I really *didn't* need to worry, but I was still a little concerned,

JON, DOUG AND JOCELYN ON CALIFORNIA BEACH (2004)

after his five years of college, about Jon's preparation for the "real" world.

During the summer of 2005, he had interviewed over the phone for the part-time youth director position in Ogden, Utah. Ascension Lutheran Church couldn't afford to fill a full-time position. Jon "blew away" the interviewers. He went to work in Utah in the fall. Since the position was without benefits, Jon found a second job at the Weber County Library. We were able to read about Jon's youth group activities in the Ascension Lutheran newsletter. We heard more by phone as he described the difficulties of gaining the trust of teenagers and trying to develop a Christian community.

Jon spent that last Christmas with his sister Jocelyn in California. He wanted to be in a warm place to run as well as to spend time with his two-year-old niece, Audrey, and meet his six-month-old nephew, Charlie. Jon promised to be home in Minnesota for his twenty-fourth birthday in March and to help us pack up the house. Linda and I were moving into a townhouse in Stillwater. I called it "assisted living." Someone else would cut the grass and shovel the snow. I could sell my lawnmowers and yard tools.

As planned, Jon came home for his birthday in March 2006. While at home he quietly packed up his bedroom and most of his carefully maintained athletic equipment, Matchbox cars, action figures, and Legos. I sensed that he was upset that we were selling his boyhood home, but we didn't talk about it.

I have been moved to passionately idealize my son. I was nearly two generations older than him, and I sometimes could hardly believe that he genuinely wanted to spend time with me. I missed much of his brief life. When Jon was growing up at home, I worked too many hours, made too many trips away from home, and said "yes" too many times to activities that took me away from my family. I now remember with painful regret many missed opportunities to spend time with my son,

JON'S TWENTY-FOURTH BIRTHDAY, SUNDAY, MARCH 5, 2006.

to play games, build things, just sit quietly together, or camp under the stars. I didn't visit Jon in Guatemala, in Utah, or in Idaho. I didn't share Jon's love for the mountains and we never did a western "road trip" together. If only I could do it all over.

Many years earlier, I felt a similar regret that I didn't spend much time with my dad when he was ill with cancer, and I was not with him when he died at home, a week before his fifty-sixth birthday. I was twenty-six years old, at the U.S. Naval Submarine School in New London, Connecticut, when I got the call. After his funeral I wrote a letter to my dad telling him many things I never said to him when we were together. Writing a letter to him helped me to express the pain I felt losing him, so I decided to write a similar letter to my son. I began with words of love.

Dear Jon:

You were with us for such a short time. How I miss you. You made my life whole. I loved you beyond measure. Your brief life and your remarkable qualities are now an inspiration to me...

I reminded Jon that he was not perfect.

But you were human. You were often stubborn, impatient and ornery. Sometimes you were testy and unapproachable, particularly when you were going deep before a competitive running event. During those times, we dared not talk to you. Sometimes you reduced your mother to tears with your grumpy attitude. I remember when you were in college and developed a persistent hamstring injury. Your performance and speed declined and your frustration and post-race grumpiness increased. My heart ached for you...

I thought about how often he took on difficult challenges.

I know you were close to God in the wilderness. I didn't know you were climbing rugged mountains—alone. Did you know how risky that was? You always had confidence in your ability to accomplish tough goals...a notable strength of yours, and perhaps, your fatal flaw...

But, still, he was extraordinary.

In my heart of hearts, when I remember your remarkable life, I am content to idealize you. You earned it. I often saw you change sadness into joy. You were with us for only a fleeting moment. But in that time, you made a difference. You were a gift to us from God...

His strong faith surpassed mine.

It's a nagging regret that I remember having only one discussion about theology with you—a religion major. I should have asked you to explain the Holy Trinity to me. One of my happiest memories is our dinner conversation when I turned to you and said, "Jon, when I get to heaven, I'm going to ask God why She didn't do a better job in creation. Why is our world so full of suffering, chaos, tribal warfare, and violence?"

You thought for a minute, as you often did, and responded, "Dad, isn't that kind of arrogant?"

"Perhaps," I quickly said, "but I think I deserve to know. And by the way, if there is no heaven, I'm really going to be mad!"

I remembered our last conversation.

I will hold in my heart forever the last words we spoke. In the summer of 2006, you returned again to Luther Heights Bible Camp. You called me in the evening of Wednesday, July 12, 2006. Once again, you were having a great time at camp, but thought it was probably your last summer in Idaho. You said you knew it was hard for us to be so far from you, but you loved the mountains, living out west, and your work as a youth minister.

"That's okay, son," I said. "It's called leaving home. We all leave home."

You said you needed to go, to prepare for the next day at camp. We said goodbye, and I love you. That was the last time I ever spoke with you.

I finished with an expression of admiration and closed with the words Jon always put at the end of his letters, *Peace and Love, Dad*

Chapter 21

THE FRENZY

THURSDAY, JULY 26, 2007, SAWTOOTH CITY, IDAHO

We knew that when we found Jon's body there would be a frenzy, a brief period of renewed media interest. I looked forward to that renewed interest and an opportunity for me to talk about my son and to tell people what a remarkable young man he was. It also allowed me to talk about the Jon Francis Foundation and the good works we hoped to accomplish.

Jeff and I spent the entire day and evening of July 26 returning phone calls, providing media interviews, and sending out the press releases we'd prepared. Locked in my bedroom, away from the grandchildren, I spoke with about thirty reporters across the country from newspapers, radio, and television. Many were dedicated journalists who had been with us since July 15, 2006. I spoke with Mary Divine of the *Pioneer Press*, Dana Dugan of the *Idaho Mountain Express*, Mark Brouwer of the *Stillwater Courier*, Kevin Giles of the *Star Tribune*, Glen Barbour of KSTP-TV in St. Paul, and Alyson Outen of KTVB-TV in Boise. They had become like old friends. I also spoke with many media newcomers to the saga. We sent each of them a news release and a photograph of the location on the Grand Mogul where Jon's remains were found.

LOCATION OF JON'S REMAINS ON THE NORTH FACE OF THE GRAND MOGUL

FOR IMMEDIATE RELEASE
July 27, 2007
Contact: Jeff Hasse, Director JFF
jonfrancisfoundation@gmail.com

Identity of the remains of Jon Francis has been confirmed by dental records. Position of the remains of Jon Francis established on the north face of the Grand Mogul in the Sawtooth Mountains of Idaho.

Today, the human remains brought down from Grand Mogul were confirmed by dental records to be those of Jon Francis of Stillwater, Minnesota. Further, the search manager who coordinated the family-led search, Jeff Hasse, president of Search, Rescue

144

and Recovery Resources of Minnesota, is currently conducting a reconstruction of Jon's descent from Grand Mogul, which resulted in his fatal accident.

The reconstruction will become part of the Jon Francis search case file, which has attracted national attention within the search and rescue community because of its complexity, large scale, and length. The Jon Francis Foundation, established this year to honor Jon's memory, will compile the extensive information and lessons learned from his search and make it available to search and rescue organizations and law enforcement.

Jon's father, David Francis, says; "We launched the Jon Francis Foundation (JFF) to bring some good out of his loss and to make a difference in people's lives, just as Jon did. JFF hopes to advocate for wilderness safety and education in order to help reduce incidents of loss. In addition, JFF will embrace a mission to be a resource to the search and rescue community and to families and individuals searching for a lost loved one."

Please visit www.jonfrancis.org for more information.

On Saturday, July 28, I received a call from the Idaho mortician asking me if we had made a decision to have Jon's remains cremated. Alarmed, I repeated our instructions to him that we expected him to safeguard Jon's remains until we found all of them possible. After that, we would call him. When I got off the phone, I immediately called the coroner, Vicki Armbruster, and asked her to help us keep him on task. She said she would.

After weeks of planning, grieving, and climbing, Linda and I teetered on the edge of mental and physical exhaustion. Utah friends Joanna and Cecilia came to Idaho to be with us again and to provide some food, help, and comfort. While Jeff was working on a further recovery plan, we decided to drive to Boise to take refuge for a few days with our cousins Wayne and Sue. We had stayed with them several times during our journey of sorrow, and they had provided a safe harbor in our storm.

On Monday, July 30, while we were in Boise, the coroner called. The Idaho mortician had called asking for her written approval to cremate Jon's remains. Vicki was now as alarmed as I was. She recommended that we "remove" Jon's remains from him and place them with Jones and Casey Funeral Home in Challis, Idaho. Desperate, I agreed, drafted a letter of authorization, had it notarized, and faxed it to her at the Custer County Sheriff's Office.

Linda and I held hands and cried. Later that day, we were relieved to learn from Vicki that Jon's remains were placed in the care of the funeral director at Jones and Casey in Challis, Idaho.

The time had come to return Jon to Minnesota—to bring Jon home. I could not allow his remains to stay in Idaho any longer. I requested that the two funeral directors, Tammy in Idaho and Nickie in Minnesota, immediately arrange air transportation to carry Jon back to Minnesota.

Chapter 22

BRINGING JON HOME

"When he has found it, he lays it on his shoulders and
rejoices. And when he comes home, he calls together his
friends and his neighbors, saying to them 'Rejoice with me,
for I have found my sheep that was lost.'"

LUKE 15: 5-6 (NRSV)

WEDNESDAY, AUGUST 1, 2007, IDAHO

This would be the second birthday Linda would have to spend in Idaho, mourning her son's loss and hoping to bring him home. This was the day we had relentlessly striven toward for a year; the day when we would transport Jon's body back to Minnesota. But Linda could not bring herself to board the flight with me. She stayed in Idaho in the comfort of Jocelyn and her grandchildren. It was up to me to make the trip.

The Idaho funeral director had flown with Jon on Salmon Airlines to Boise. I met Tammy at the gate and we talked for a while. It turned out that she was born in North Dakota and had lived and attended college in Minnesota. She understood why we were taking this step and knew we relied on her to safeguard and transport all future remains that still might be found.

I boarded Northwest Airlines for Minneapolis, watching the baggage loading conveyor to see how they would handle my son. I was assured that the package would be clearly labeled "HUMAN REMAINS," and that baggage handlers were trained to give them special care. But I never saw the package. On the flight home, I read *Lament for a Son* a third time. This time, I was able to hold back my tears.

When I arrived at Twin Cities International around 5:30 p.m., I was greeted by Jay, a limo driver sent by Nickie, the Stillwater funeral director. Stepping outside the airport, I was assaulted by a wall of heat and humidity. Living in Idaho for the summer, I had forgotten how humid the Midwest could be in August. Jay drove around the terminal to the VIP baggage area. I remained inside the air-conditioned limo while he went inside. He returned with a box.

I was stunned and horrified when I saw how small the package was. These were not how I'd pictured "remains." These were fragments! This is all that is left of my son — a few bones in a cardboard box!

After Jay placed the cardboard shipping container in the backseat of the car, his pager rang. He read the page and turned to me, saying, "The 35W Bridge has just collapsed."

In my horror, the first thought that came into my head was the paragraph on transportation that I had repeated over and over for months on the campaign trail: "We are under-investing in road and bridge maintenance and construction. In Minnesota today, there are over 800 bridges that have exceeded their 'span of life' and safe use." Later, I was reminded of how connected we are when I learned that my friend and business colleague, Peter Hausmann, was among the thirteen killed that day.

Fortunately, our drive to Simonet Funeral Home in Stillwater did not require crossing the 35W Bridge. I told Jay that I wanted to carry our son's remains into the funeral home. But I was not prepared for the stark horror of cradling my son's body, his bones, in the small cardboard box.

Melissa was already at the funeral home. When she saw what I was carrying, her beautiful face turned into a mask of agony. "Dad, he's in a box!" She, too, felt the cruel reality of what had happened to her only brother.

We were directed to a room where I placed the box on the bier, a pedestal that supports a casket. With tears of pain and love, Melissa placed a rosary on Jon's box. Wrapped in a side-by-side embrace, we stood in silence.

At home that evening, I called Linda in Idaho to let her know I'd arrived and to wish her a happy birthday. How unnatural that sounded. She planned to eat dinner at the Smiley Creek Café with Jocelyn and her family. I ate alone that night.

The following morning, I met with Father Jerry and Nickie at the funeral home to talk about Jon's funeral and burial arrangements. In the now familiar script, I said, "Nickie, please safeguard our son's remains until we finish our recovery work and decide on final arrangements. We are going back on the mountain to search for more of Jon's remains."

Nickie told me about above-ground columbariums in Stillwater, one at a cemetery near our home, that we could consider for Jon's ashes. Linda and I had discussed how Jon would approve of cremation as environmentally responsible. Rutherford Cemetery, established in 1850, was about four blocks, a short walk, from our house. I had driven past there hundreds of times, but had never stopped. It always reminded me of boot hill, an old western graveyard on a hill at the edge of town.

I drove straight there and picked up a brochure at the gate. The pamphlet described the history of the cemetery and mentioned that it was managed by an association. A quote on the brochure read:

A line of lofty cedars, nearly as old as the burial ground below, stands sentinel duty. When the wind blows, as it almost always does on Rutherford Hill, the cedars hum a requiem.

I walked into the burial ground and read some of the gravestones. Many of the pioneer families of Stillwater and their young children were buried here, including William Rutherford, who donated the land for the cemetery and died in 1888 at age sixty-five. I read other markers.

Liberty Newman, 1821-1876, fifty-five years
George Rutherford, 1859-1884, twenty-five years old
Stillman Masterman, 1877, nine years old
Martha Masterman, 1865, five years old
Ira Holden, 1876, nine months old

Chiseled in stone was evidence that the young can die, that many other families lost children even much younger than Jon. I was drawn to a lone columbarium standing behind cemetery hill, on flat ground, facing a wall constructed of boulders, and surrounded by green space. The horizon was abundant with trees with a white-framed non-denominational church to the north, holding a cross high on its roof. In the backyard of the church was an inviting playground area and fire pit surrounded by benches. A canoe sat nearby. I assumed the area was created for the youth of the congregation.

This place felt like an island sanctuary in a sea of noise, traffic, commerce, and unceasing human activity—a fitting place to lay Jon to rest. But Linda and I needed to make this important decision together.

During the dinner conversation with family friends that evening, I was distracted with thoughts of returning to the mountain to continue the search. I did not want to leave any part of my son on that mountain.

My heart was heavy with dread as I boarded the plane back to Idaho.

Chapter 23

LAKE JON

"The Lord is my shepherd, I shall not want. He makes me lie down in green pastures; he leads me beside still waters; he restores my soul."

PSALM 23 (NRSV)

AUGUST 2007, IDAHO

On Monday, August 5, members of the Sawtooth Mountain Guides ascended the crack system above the gulley where Jon's remains had been recovered. They found Jon's black-and-yellow backpack and some bone fragments. In the pack, they found his clothing, his car keys, the ten essentials, and his camera. After we retrieved Jon's camera from the sheriff's office, we eagerly downloaded the memory chip into our computer. There, as if a gift to us from our son, were the pictures Jon took while standing on the summit.

I was now familiar with the view, one that I had seen twice as I stood on the top of the Grand Mogul. But now, I imagined I was seeing it through my son's eyes.

After lingering for some time, magically seeing God's creation through Jon's eyes, I called the Custer County sheriff to ask about his

VIEW FROM SUMMIT, TAKEN BY JON ON SATURDAY, JULY 15, 2006.

plans to continue the search for Jon's remains. He said that his deputy would be contacting me. I placed several messages on the deputy's voicemail. I called Erik Leidecker to see if he had heard from the sheriff's office. He had not.

I don't know why I expected the sheriff to keep his word this time. On August 8, two weeks after our meeting with Custer County law enforcement authorities, we still hadn't heard of any official activity. Custer County never kept their promise to organize any other recovery effort.

The first time I had climbed into the bowl on the north face under the summit of the Grand Mogul, I was struck by its sheer ugliness. The bowl of shattered rock is a boulder junkyard strewn with deteriorated granite that continuously falls off the face of the mountain. After my sadness and disgust slowly waned, I thought of the mountain mystique that I'd been ambushed by in July 2006. This was not a romantic, snow-covered, alpine peak. This was not Shangri-La. It was an ugly rock pile. Don't tell me that my son died in an enchanted realm, or that he died in a place where he wanted to be. Jon chose the most direct and, tragically, the most difficult route off the mountain because he wanted to catch the three p.m. shuttle and get back to camp.

Again, I voiced my lament: "God, where were you? Why didn't you guide my son's feet safely off this mountain?"

I called Erik and asked him if he would climb again. SMG went up on August 15; Johnny Unser and Taz went with them. They found no additional bones or fragments. Jon's remains were found in a snow-pack, which since July had slowly melted away. I spent a day in the bowl with my son-in-law Doug and Al Jones, owner of the Smiley Creek Café. We chopped and dug with a pickaxe and shovel through other snow packs in the faint hope that we might find more scattered fragments.

I climbed, stumbled, and searched around in that rock pile several more times. Once with Ann Moser from Forensic Dogs of Idaho and her canine Watson, and my final trip with my neighbor Marlies and her search dog China.

By late August, after several climbs on the north face were completed, no additional remains were found. We decided that we should not risk the safety of others with further search missions. After my climb with Marlies and China, Linda and I took the *Searching for Jon* boat out of the water.

The final hunt for Jon's remains was led, at my request, by Bob Meredith and a six-person team from the Idaho Mountain Search and Rescue Unit. They covered the east face of the north ridge. They ascended from the bowl up to 9,000 feet. But they found nothing else.

On the north side of the Grand Mogul rests a small, unnamed lake. The water is tranquil and transparent. In July 2006, when I first began studying maps of the Sawtooth Mountains, I was struck by the curiosity

that the lake had no name. That summer, we began to refer to it as
"Lake Jon." It became a landmark, a campsite, and a rendezvous point
during our searches.

On August 26, I camped with Ken Schulte and Bruce Engelby of
the Mighty Ascension Search Team at Lake Jon on the evening before
they left. They had spent two days searching in the steep crevices high
up on the north face. I brought them supper—chili and beer—and
camped with them, holding my own quiet vigil and bidding farewell to
my son in view of the summit of the Grand Mogul.

By now, Luther Heights Bible Camp was closing their summer ses-
sions. Many of the counselors who had worked, hiked, climbed, prayed,
and played with Jon came to say goodbye to us in Sawtooth City. Ian,
who had created the amazing postcard painting, came to see us before
returning to college. Maren came to tell us that, after a brief return to
her home in Minnesota, she was going on a mission trip to Europe.
Samantha (Sam) Butler, who had climbed with Jon, came and gave us a
copy of her short story called "Bittersweet" about her and Jon and the
lasting influence that his presence made in her life. She was going back
to college at Boise State.

Caryl Bauwens and her parents came to say goodbye. Caryl was
Jon's girlfriend for many years. She lived in Boise and went to college
at the University of Idaho. We had met her in Stillwater years earlier
when she came to Minnesota to "meet the parents." Caryl had been a
counselor at Luther Heights and had climbed the Sawtooths with Jon.
The Bauwens thoughtfully established and funded a Luther Heights
Bible Camp Scholarship in Jon's name. Caryl gave us a letter. Here is
some of what she wrote:

> Jon was my first serious boyfriend; he was my first everything. In
> the deepest sense he was my soulmate. After meeting him and
> letting him love me the way he did, I will never be the same.

He never hesitated in speaking his mind...Our conversations had substance; he made me think about bigger things while also making sure I appreciated the little moments. After every conversation I had with Jon I left feeling like I knew myself better...I believed I had the power to be a better human being.

He lived this way: Jon wanted to know everything and his irresistible curiosity...and love of life [were] contagious. What scares me the most is that I will never meet another person like Jon. I'm scared that no one will ever measure up.

Jocelyn organized a thank-you and farewell dinner for the Sawtooth Mountain Guides. Over the many months in our search for Jon, Erik Leidecker and his guides were our rock. They not only provided the best talent, knowledge, hope, and results, the Sawtooth Mountain Guides were the ones who found our son. We met them for dinner at the Redfish Lake Lodge. There was no charge for the food. Jeff Clegg, Lodge owner and friend, paid for it.

That evening, Erik mentioned that the bill he had sent to Custer County for his services had been returned to him unpaid. Linda told him to send it to us.

"No. We were working for the sheriff, and he is responsible for the bill," Erik said.

We left it to him to settle. Some of the SMG men and their spouses were with us that evening at dinner. These young men and others had, for months in bitter cold, stifling heat, and often unpredictable weather, repeatedly risked their personal safety to help us find our son. Not since my days as a submarine officer had I felt such depth of admiration and gratitude toward a crew of men.

That summer, we made one more trip across Redfish Lake. Linda had commissioned Wayne at the Smiley Creek Café to construct a sign that we could place on the shore of Lake Jon. Wayne created an attractive, rustic marker for us that fit with the environment.

Linda, Jocelyn, Doug, and I, along with the kids, hiked to Lake Jon. Doug carried Audrey. Jocelyn carried Charlie. I carried the Lake Jon sign. It was a warm, clear September day. We ate lunch on the shore. Doug, Audrey, and I then dug a hole and secured the sign in the ground. Whether the Lake Jon marker will remain there for long, we don't know. But our broken hearts remain there, forever.

THE LAKE JON MARKER (2007)

Chapter 24

GO FORTH, JON

Linda and I left Sawtooth City and drove back to Minnesota. We arrived home on September 7 to be immediately confronted with many mournful choices, decisions no parent should ever have to make.

Jeff Hasse had encouraged us to have Jon's remains examined by a forensic anthropologist. He thought it was important to have this information as part of the accident investigation. I resisted; I was weary of having my son's remains carted around. Frankly, after the Idaho episode, I was worried that they might get lost.

Reluctantly, Linda and I agreed to the examination by a forensic anthropologist in St. Paul. Jeff asked me if we wanted a copy of the report. I declined. I only wanted answers to two questions: What caused Jon's death? And, did he linger and suffer?

Jeff confirmed that Jon died of "blunt force trauma" to his head. He fell a very long way. Jeff explained that the re-growth of bone takes place quickly as an injured body tries to heal itself, and there was no evidence of bone re-growth. Jon's death was immediate.

Linda and I chose cremation and visited the funeral home to select an urn. The viewing room, full of caskets and urns, was suffocating. I felt close to a panic attack. We chose a wooden box made of Minnesota cherry to hold Jon's ashes. To be inscribed on the box, we selected words from the Celtic Funeral Service.

Go forth Jon, son, brother, friend,
servant of God, Christian soul.

Next, we met with the director of the Rutherford Cemetery Association and chose the niche where we would place the inscribed box. The niche, Jon's tomb, faced west toward the setting sun.

A friend suggested that we scatter some of Jon's ashes on the Grand Mogul.

"No." Linda said. "There's enough of Jon on that mountain."

With the help of Father Jerry and Ascension's music director, we selected a traditional Celtic (Old Irish) funeral service with scripture, poems, readings, and hymns. The ancient Celts spiritual traditions were rooted in nature. We wanted the funeral to honor Jon, pay tribute to his heritage as a great-great grandson of an Irish immigrant, and celebrate Jon's love for God's creation and devotion to the environment, as well as his deep faith, joy, and selfless ministry to others.

I called my friends at the newspapers in Stillwater, St. Paul, Minneapolis, Ketchum, and Ogden to ask them to inform the community about Jon's burial service. For days I read, with tears of love and respect, Jon's papers and poems from college to select a few for the funeral service. I asked Jon's sisters, his godparents, and his friend Alex if they would read a few of them with me.

Tuesday, October 9, 2007, was a colder-than-usual, breezy, gray day in Stillwater, Minnesota. The Francis family gathered at Ascension Church. But we were incomplete; Jon was not there. For a second time, we sat in the library until Father Jerry came for us to start the procession into the church.

Despite the fact that it was a weekday, the church was full of Jon's friends and loved ones, including one dog sitting near the back. Jim Hanley was there with his dog, Shania. Their presence felt particularly fitting; Jim and Shania had been with us from the beginning of the search for Jon.

The lack of sunshine that day kept the church darker than usual. Candles flickered on the altar at the front. Carrying Jon's wooden ossuary, I led the family into the church, following the cross. As we processed, Father Jerry read from Isaiah 55: "For you shall go out in joy, and be led back in peace; the mountains and the hills before you shall burst into song and all the trees of the field shall clap their hands…"

At the front of the congregation I placed the inscribed urn on a table near the pulpit. I sat down next to Linda and our daughters in the front pew.

The music, scripture, and prayers of the Celtic funeral service provided a sense of solace and poignancy as everyone present celebrated and honored Jon's spirit as well as grieved for the lost life of our precious son.

I stood to read Jon's words, "Make connections; let rip with joy…," that so perfectly reflected his joyful love of nature: "My bursting forth takes the form of celebration, of grace, of awe and wonder, of humility and of thanksgiving. I am celebrating the goodness of nature. I am thankful for the goodness of the created world. I do not know why, but I am closer to God when I am outside…I give glory to God for her abundant creation. There is goodness all round. There is goodness deep within."

Some of Jon's favorite poems were interspersed with beautiful scripture and music. Robin stood to read Walt Whitman's "The Runner." Melissa read "Leaves of Grass."

Jon's friend Alex read a poem that Linda had shared with Jon from a book called *Stars in Your Bones: Emerging Signposts on Our Spiritual Journeys.* The poem was one of Jon's favorites and movingly reflected the kind of love Jon gave so freely.

Biodance

by Alla Bozarth

everything bears the property of Love

Sitting on a rock in the Salmon River
watching first leaves fall.

From sunhigh mountain treetops
upstream the rapids carry
old branches to the sea,
their leaves landlocked already.

Why so soon?
Not soon at all—
your time is complete.
And so is mine.

You rest in sunlight
before transforming
into earth and air.

You dissolve your leafy form
and recompose into a thousand bodies.

Nothing ever ends.
Everything is always
        beginning.

Shall I find myself tomorrow
shining in a waterdrop
on a piece of moss
on the bark of a tree
that once was you?

Green into burntred,
old leaf, our biodance began
millennia ago, but today
I am glad to see you clearly

for the first time
with just these eyes,
my changing
partner!

Your bronze body
Turns to powder
with a crack
beneath my foot.

Part of you has already become me.
You are on your new way.

You will be back.
And so will I.
So will I.

I was drawn almost into a state of euphoria—a fullness of feeling. I was carried along by the beauty of the poetry and the music—all this for Jon, to honor him.

Father Jerry's homily began, "The Celts believed God was in everything. In a way, Jon is part of creation now. Every time you see the sunrise, the moon coming up over the water, the leaves changing in the fall, and new flowers in the spring, just as surely you're seeing Jon…"

The Commendation ended with:

Go forth, Jon,
son, brother, friend, servant of God, Christian soul,
in the name of God who knows you
and with the blessing of those
who love you.

As the recessional hymn started, I walked over, picked up, and cradled the Minnesota ossuary box containing Jon's remains. As I turned to leave, I was suddenly overcome with the finality of the walk ahead of me and tears streamed from my eyes. This was the first time I had broken down in public. I blessed my son again with fierce tears as I walked down the aisle, passing the mournful faces all around me.

Jon's godparents, John and Coralie, drove us to Rutherford Hill. I sat motionless in the backseat, tightly holding the wooden box. When we arrived at the cemetery, the niche was open. Our friend Mark Schwantes was already there, standing like a sentry, holding the cross, near the gray granite columbarium.

Mourners gathered around the family in front of the niche. But I couldn't let go; I continued to grip the box. Father Jerry gently told me it was time to place the box in the marble vault. Finally, I carefully placed my son's remains inside his tomb and led the assembly in reading his committal:

Jonathan
I bless you; I release you.
I set you free; I set me free.
I let you be; I let me be.

I sprinkled a handful of sand over the box. Linda and I had collected three bags of sand from the lakes Jon loved and once played near—Lake Michigan, Redfish Lake, and Little Carnelian Lake. The rest of the mourners formed a solemn line and each, in turn, sprinkled sand on Jon's consecrated, final resting place. As the slow procession of mourners walked by, I thought back to our first vigil held in view of the Grand Mogul, and my first farewell to our son. "Jon, I love you. Jon, I miss you. You are gone. You have passed over. My soul is torn. I will lift you up and place you into the arms of God."

I turned and saw the caretaker standing motionless and alone on the hill amidst all the old gravestones. I motioned for him and he came forward and sealed, then fastened the door shut.

Everyone huddled in the cold wind. And just as the poem promised: "When the wind blows, as it almost always does on Rutherford Hill, the cedars hummed a requiem."

Linda and I hugged as many people as we could in the somber gathering. I lingered. I didn't want to leave; I wanted to stay with Jon. But Linda and I did leave; we went forth to live the remainder of our lives, and to somehow learn to bear the loneliness, the emptiness, the hole in our hearts that is life without our son Jon.

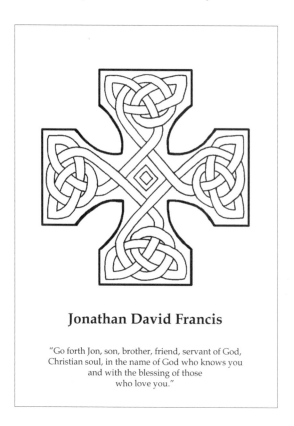

Jonathan David Francis

"Go forth Jon, son, brother, friend, servant of God,
Christian soul, in the name of God who knows you
and with the blessing of those
who love you."

Chapter 25

FAITH OF OUR CHILDREN

In the months following Jon's funeral many friends sent us letters with memories and stories about Jon. Jocelyn wrote about her special relationship with Jon, saying, "A big part of me died on July 15th, 2006. Jon was my baby brother but I looked up to him and I think in some ways we completed each other—I was put on earth to loosen him up and he was put on earth to mellow me out. There was mutual respect, admiration, and love between us—he frequently amazed me with his wise-beyond-his-years perspective and thoughtfulness. Jon and I shared a love of many things—music, food (okay, candy), sports, hiking, camping, the Spanish language and culture, traveling, thrift shopping, and just plain having fun. I find myself listening to our mutually adored bands on a daily basis and I doubt I will ever be able to make it through the *Landslide* by Stevie Nicks without crying. It was first recorded by Fleetwood Mac and then the Dixie Chicks (yes, Jon and I both LOVE the Dixie Chicks). I miss him but listening to the music we love fills me with his spirit and energy."

Melissa wrote, "Jon was the hero of our family. His triumphs were our triumphs—his running prowess, good grades, and spiritual pursuits. Eerily, he was on another spiritual quest when he climbed to the peak of the Grand Mogul. In my mind, Jon joined a long line of Saints who sought a relationship with God in the wilderness. As his sister, it comforts me to remember that Jon lived life as a kind and spiritual person. After his death we held him up as our family saint. I am sure it would make him squirm for us to deify him. He was human with many traits of an idealistic twenty-four-year-old man. I feel closer to him, remembering that humanness. Jon knew the importance of being close to family and being kind to children — his greatest legacy in my view. He hugged me when I was sad. He wrote long and thoughtful birthday cards and relished my children's birthday parties. In our last picture of Jon, his image is captured in the corner of the frame (on the Redfish Lake shuttle boat). His head was tilted down, eyes hidden by the brim of his baseball cap; but his handsome profile was visible with his long, unruly left sideburn. But I will place a different picture on my bedside table, one of Jon lunging down the wet Slip and Slide at Katie's fifth birthday party, and I will remember my brother with love and thankfulness."

Robin was sixteen when Jon was born, so she was away at college while he was growing up. She wrote, "In some ways, Jon followed in my footsteps. We both had great affection for the Spanish culture and language. I spent a semester in Madrid and a year in Bolivia with the Aymara and Quechua people. Jon spent a semester in Guatemala and learned about sustainable farming. But Jon was his own person, drawn to live in the West and near mountains, while I lived in New York and Washington, DC. As part of the search for Jon, I discovered more about what was important to him, how many mountains he climbed, storms he weathered, and people he touched. After losing him, I learned about his spiritual depth and what was in his heart."

Jon's boss, Laura, at Luther Heights shared her memories of Jon. She talked about his sense of fun and how good he was with the kids — dancing, singing, being able to reach even the toughest of kids.

Laura described how warmly Jon greeted her when he came back to Luther Heights that last summer (2006).

She said, "He moved differently, looked different to me somehow. It became apparent to me within that first day that he found his stride. He was comfortable in his own skin. He had come into his own. There was a new confidence in the way he spoke, the way he moved, how he shared with others who he was and what he believed. It was a marvelous thing to see—he felt so new to me, yet he was still the Jon I had known all along—intensely curious about religion, his life of faith, the world, and the big questions that involve all of those elements and many more. Over the years we had enjoyed many conversations on these topics. I was excited to hear him talk about his potential next moves in ministry, including seminary somewhere in his future. He never knew that I would begin study at Luther Seminary in St. Paul, Minnesota, after that summer. I waited until the end of the summer to tell the staff so that my leaving wouldn't be a distraction to the lives of staff and campers. I am sad that we did not get to talk about our common passion that had us both eyeing ordained ministry."

Jon's friend Alex was like a daughter to Linda and me. When I asked her to write about what Jon meant to her, she described Jon as an "athlete of love." I was moved by her connecting his passion for running with his capacity to love. I could always see that Jon was wired to run, and he was also wired to love.

Alex wrote: "Jon's running was impenetrable to me as much as I sought to participate in and offer support to him. I have grown to see his athleticism not so much as an isolated and extraordinary gift, but rather as an extension or manifestation of his character. He poured out discipline, hard work, patience, persistence, hope, and grace into many areas of his life, especially his relationships...Jon stepped into our house with a sense of grace and courage...with his lighthearted playfulness as he jumped on my brother's back, told silly and absurd jokes, danced through our kitchen to his own music, and simply laughed out loud. Jon poured and oozed and hugged the love of God onto us with kindness and gentleness...He was a pastor, a healer, a friend, and a kind of athlete of love to us. I don't think I have ever loved or been more fully loved by anyone."

Jon's capacity to love was inextricably connected to his strong faith. When Jon was fourteen, he talked his way into the Ascension Episcopal confirmation class filled with older kids. He shared his personal testimony with the youth minister and assistant priest, the Reverend LeeAnne Watkins. He passionately told her, "I would like to publicly affirm my faith and have my church affirm me."

One of LeeAnne's requirements for confirmation was to link up each student with an adult mentor who was a member of Ascension Church. Jon chose John Steffen, an insurance agent and a former college football coach. At that time, John was dealing with a difficult personal issue that he shared with Jon. The mentoring process became mutual as Jon became a natural mentor to John, accepting him without judgment. John said that our teenager helped him to more fully live his faith, find a deeper understanding of God, and learn how to treat others with the kind of acceptance and unconditional love that Jon demonstrated.

The Reverend LeeAnne Watkins sent me a copy of the homily she wrote the day of Jon's funeral.

Written the day we buried Jon

My heart hurts. I helped bury a young man today. I stood in the autumn wind and watched as his father placed the small box which contained what was left of his son into a vault. The boy's name was Jon Francis. He was the quietest member of my youth group out at Ascension Church in Stillwater. Jon and his family were very good to me when I took the job out there, fresh out of seminary.

Today, I kept thinking of all the Thursday night youth groups, church lock-ins, and the trips to a summer cabin singing, "Bye, Bye, Miss American Pie." I remembered him playing chess with his mentor at the House of Prayer retreat. I thought of what a leader he was in the Teens Encounter Christ weekends, he seemed so steady and solid and prayerful. He laughed often. . . .

"Today I thought of the vacation Bible school we did with homeless youth in Minneapolis, and how even though he was so small in stature the children climbed all over him, and he was tender and gentle with them, so attentive and sensitive; and it was obvious that he had a gift in working with children.

I thought today of how he has been the only young person I've sponsored for confirmation as young as sixteen. He wanted to be confirmed, and so I made him sit down with me and explain why . . . that day he started talking about God and just couldn't stop and one-and-a-half-hours later we were both in tears at how wondrous and lavish our God is. I have rarely seen such depth of faith in anyone, no matter their age. Jon's heart was as open to God as God's was to him. A beautiful thing.

And today we buried him, finally, beautifully, each of us sprinkling over him a handful of sand from one of his favorite lakes. And my heart hurts. It hurts because I'm now a parent and the thought of losing my child makes my blood turn cold. It hurts because Jon had such promise as a youth minister, a pastor, and a theologian. It hurts because, well, because I opened my heart to him and my life is changed because of him, and now he's dead.

I can fret and try to protect those I love, but I will fail. Life is fragile. Knowledge of that is terrifying. There's a good case to be made for never opening a heart to love, because it hurts. The risk is great. An open heart is an unprotected heart. But love we do, because God is love. And God first loved us. And God is in us. And there are times of great joy and laughter and amazement when you love with open hearts. Jon's life and his death teach that. Love is worth it.

And that's what church is. Jon was giving his life for this idea, because he understood what church is, people bound together in love by a loving God. Today I saw those youth group members all grown up, stuffed into suits and wiping their eyes. I saw elders climbing the stairs to Eucharist. I heard children singing, *"there is wideness to God's mercy."* I saw church. Such brave lovers. Such holiness. Jon's people, chock full of love, living with open hearts, and showing up even when, especially when, our hearts hurt, and loving still.

LeeAnne is right. An open heart is an unprotected heart and life is fleeting and fragile. But love is hardy and enduring.

In the years since I lost my son, people have asked me how I'm doing. I distilled my responses into short sentences:

"I'm okay. But I miss Jon."

"I'm learning to live with a hole in my heart."

"The Jon Francis Foundation gives me a sense of purpose."

My calendar is now populated with sad anniversaries: March 5, Jon's birthday and the last time he was with us at home; July 15, the day he died on the Grand Mogul; July 24, the day most of his remains were found; August 1, the day I brought Jon home on Linda's birthday; September 9, his memorial service at Ascension church; and October 9, 2007, the date we laid Jon to rest.

The day after Jon's funeral, I began to write. I wanted to put my pain on paper as an act of grief and healing. I was increasingly inspired by my son's brief life. As I wrote, I often cried. I desperately wanted others to know that an uncommon young man named Jon Francis once lived and loved among us.

Jon loved to dance. His friend Britt said that Jon often brought a boom box to high school and organized small dance parties during lunch. But Jon also understood the "divine" dance. Early in his life he caught and felt a deep faith in a creator god. He appeared to know about the Holy Trinity even before he was potty-trained. He "danced" with God and became a steward of God's mysteries and creation. Jon was a hearer of the Word and a doer, a questioner, and a seeker. In a college paper, Jon wrote about a time of questioning in his faith:

I know that God may be around but I don't understand why things are a certain way. Why couldn't the earth, life, be different? It is not the best of all possible worlds. Is it our life as humans to keep failing with our responsibility?

I grow tired of failing. I grow tired of trying. It does seem like I may never do enough. Does God ever intervene anymore?

I believe that we should question God if we do not fully understand. But I am not fully sure about what my questioning and thinking has done for me. Why is God not trustworthy? Is it only our own fault because of the way we've made the world? The dance and the circle of questions continue. I feel a sense of injustice, uncertainty, and a longing to reach points of resolution.

If we keep demanding that God yield up His answers, perhaps someday we will understand them. And then we shall be something more than clever apes, and we shall dance with God.

I will walk the middle path. There is a time to question and a time of assurance. I will walk the questioning path and I will walk the listening, praying, and receiving paths, as well.

I remain baffled by Jon's question, "Does God ever intervene anymore?" I have wondered if God is even listening.

Friends have asked me, "David, are you angry at God?" *Perhaps.* "I'm not talking to God right now." *But I haven't lost my faith.*

I turned again to my friend Father Jerry with my questioning. Jerry recalled the words of Pascal, "God did not come into the world to take away suffering; God came to lend his presence to it." He assured me that "God was present when Jon fell to his death. God was present in the volunteers who came to help. God is present in all the money that has been raised to help others in a similar circumstance. God is present in all the grief and prayers for Jon."

Even as time has passed, I continue to wonder why God didn't guide Jon's steps safely off the mountain. Jon served and glorified God with his words and deeds, his running and his climbing. I had relied on the assurances in the Bible. The Psalmist promised that angels watch over us: "For he shall give his angels charge over you, to keep you in all your ways. On their hands they will bear you up, lest you dash your foot against a stone." Losing my son jarred me from a place of assurance in my beliefs to a place of questioning.

Having no resolution, I have decided to follow in my son's footsteps—I will walk the questioning, listening, praying, and receiving paths. I will strive to accept and love, as Jon did, imperfect people, an imperfect world, and an imperfect God.

I will rely on Psalm 25:4-5.

Make me know your ways, O Lord; teach me your paths.
Lead me in your truth, and teach me,
for you are the God of my salvation;
for you I wait all day long. (NRSV)

Linda reminded me of the countless acts of kindness we received from hundreds of people who supported us in our suffering and helped us find Jon. She said, "God is in the faces, hearts, hands, and feet of others."

She writes:

From the beginning, and over the years since Jon's accident, I have felt the presence of God in the people God sent to help us. Time after time, since July 15, 2006, people came to us to offer their support.

I remember a young woman, with her two young sons, who drove for four hours from Boise, Idaho, to be with us in Stanley. She appeared to me like an angel with long golden curls. She stayed most of the day and helped us take down the tent we set up for our grandchildren—Audrey and Charlie. People came from so many places and from so far away. That was God in human skin.

The impact of Jon's accident has made me more aware and attuned to others who are going through similar suffering. I pay greater attention now when I hear news of a lost child or missing person.

Through our foundation, I hope to help others struggling with grief, despair, and unresolved loss caused by a missing loved one. Helping others may be the best help we can give ourselves.

My family is making a slow recovery. Our lives are changed forever. There are many activities I may never do again—like sending Christmas cards. They have lost their importance, take great effort, and cause great stress. I might tackle it again, someday. There are places I may never visit again. Every time I visit a familiar place, or a new place, or do a new activity, I long to have Jon with me, to share with him the wonders of life. Living is bittersweet, now.

OUR GRANDCHILDREN (L–R STEVIE, KATIE, AUDREY, TAYLOR, AND CHARLIE) 2006

Our three daughters are focusing on their own families, jobs, and lives again. For a long time it was hard to figure out where we wanted to be or what we should do. Nothing was right. Nothing fit. Slowly the rhythm of life pulled us back to a nearly normal routine and focus. We began to function again.

I will always have an empty place where Jon belongs. I will always miss him. But I'm convinced that I will see him again.

The challenge for me is to discover my new relationship with Jon and with others as I move forward on this new, un-chosen path I must take. Life continues with joys and with sorrows—our children and grandchildren; the birth of a new granddaughter, Camille; the illnesses of friends and loved ones; the rhythm of daily life. The difference now is that sorrow is a constant. Joy is welcomed, but often elusive. Life continues. We move forward.

Linda has been diligent in doing her grief work. I lag behind. I look to her wisdom. She is and has always been the glue that holds our family together.

Robin left New York and returned to Minnesota to be closer to her family. After living in Idaho for nearly two years, Jocelyn and Doug moved back to Seattle where they first met.

Melissa and Steve remained in Minnesota. Four of our six grand-children live nearby. Grandchildren are so much fun (I recommend having them first).

I am pleased and energized by the work and results of the Jon Francis Foundation. We are living our mission by working with families who are searching for lost loved ones.

In May 2008, Jim Hanley called the Jon Francis Foundation on behalf of a family in Marshall, Minnesota. Jim and his dog Shania were searching for Brandon Swanson, a nineteen-year-old college student who was missing.

Brandon's mother, Annette, gave me details. On May 14, Brandon had driven his car into a ditch by a cornfield in the early morning. He left his stuck car to walk to the nearest town. He was walking and talking on his cell phone to his father, Brian, when Brandon shouted and the phone went dead. When Annette called the sheriff's office, the dispatcher said, "Well, ma'am, your son is nineteen years old and has a right to go missing."

The family insisted that the sheriff take a missing person's report and investigate their son's disappearance. Brandon's abandoned car was located near the intersection of three Minnesota counties and the sher-iffs were having a jurisdictional dispute. The Lincoln County sheriff finally took charge and initiated a search. The sheriff had just discon-tinued the search for Brandon, having concluded that he must have fallen into the Yellow Medicine River and "would eventually surface."

The Swansons were in that dark, desperate place the Francis family inhabited in July 2006.

Linda and I drove to Marshall on Memorial Day weekend and met with the family and dozens of volunteers who were eager to continue the search. My senses were dragged back to Idaho in 2006. How similar and familiar this was! We did our best to bring hope, knowledge, and search resources. Linda comforted the family as I began to organize family and volunteers to search. We put two hundred "ground pounders" into the fields that weekend to search in a circular grid pattern within the one-mile radius from Brandon's car—his last known position. But Brandon was not found. I met with the sheriff to brief him on our presence and activities. As soon as Jeff Hasse was available, I turned the continuing search over to him.

Angered by the early resistance and lame response of law enforcement, Annette initiated a discussion with her representative in the Minnesota House of Representatives regarding the missing person's laws. The Francis' joined the Swansons in an effort to raise the awareness of elected officials regarding the lack of legal protection for missing adult children.

Missing children have been "federalized" (made a national focus of the law) because of the efforts of grieving parents like Patty and Jerry Wetterling and John Walsh. They relentlessly advocated and educated on behalf of missing children and pursued state and federal laws to guide and train law enforcement. Missing children laws, databases, and procedures are now in place in most states and at the federal level. However, missing adults (people over eighteen years old) are still a forgotten class of citizens. Missing adults fall through society's cracks.

The only law covering the missing in Minnesota was the Missing Children's Act, which was limited to those under eighteen. Unfortunately, this is a common situation throughout the country. Under current laws in more than forty states, law enforcement is not required to take a missing person's report or investigate the disappearance of anyone over eighteen.

Working alongside the Swansons, JFF set out to change this situation by engaging legislative leaders, advocacy groups, and law enforcement to revise Minnesota's missing persons' law. Brandon's Law, named in honor of Brandon Swanson, passed unanimously in the State Legislature, becoming law on July 1, 2009.

Brandon's Law replaced the outdated and inadequate Missing Children's Act and expanded the definition of a missing person to include those over eighteen years of age. Law enforcement agencies are now required to file a missing person's report "without delay" and begin an immediate investigation. We hope this is the end of first responder conversations in Minnesota that begin with, "Well, ma'am, your child is an adult and has a right to go missing."

In addition, under Brandon's Law, JFF holds a seat on a working group with the Minnesota Bureau of Criminal Apprehension and other State law enforcement leaders tasked with creating and implementing model missing person's forms and policies. This is an important opportunity for JFF to continue to be a catalyst for change.

In keeping with Jon's passion for running and his commitment to helping young people, JFF began funding camp scholarships with the proceeds from a series of races in Jon's honor.

The inaugural Jon Francis Half Marathon took place along the glistening Saint Croix River on a picture perfect Sunday morning, May 24, 2009. JFF and Stillwater community leaders organized the race with the help of more than one hundred enthusiastic volunteers and friends.

Linda and I felt a surge of emotion as hundreds of starters lined up. *Chariots of Fire* music played in the background as the announcer

MINNESOTA GOVERNOR SIGNING BRANDON'S LAW (2009)

said, "Jon Francis was an outstanding athlete, runner, and human being who represents the best that Minnesota and the village of Stillwater can raise. Today, let's remember and celebrate the life and running accomplishments of Jon Francis."

Before the race Jon's high school coach was asked by a reporter to describe Jon in one word.

"Tenacious," Christensen said without hesitation. "I could take him into a particularly hard practice and explain how important it was going to be to finish each element of the workout as strong as the previous one. I'd say, 'This can't tail off.' Jon would carry the workout all the way through. Jon came prepared every single day, and he never once complained about what we were doing. Out of the thousands of runners I've coached over the years, he's one of only a handful who drained me dry, and I mean that as a compliment. I'd come up with something to take him to the next level, and he got it. I'd give him something else, and he got that. He soaked up everything I had to offer."

The winner of the race was twenty-three-year-old Andrew Bolt, the brother of Chris Boldt, one of the "Magnificent Seven" who ran track and cross country with Jon at Stillwater High School. Bart Johnson, Jon's teammate at Augustana, took second place.

The inaugural Jon Francis Race to Alturas, organized by Jon's friends, took place in August 2009. The gorgeous day in the Sawtooths was warm and sunny, with a clear blue sky. The foot race went from Luther Heights to Lake Alturas. The race at a 7,200-foot elevation was excellent high-altitude training and a fitting tribute to Jon's life and ministry. Forty-six runners completed the course. The money raised for the Jon Francis Scholarship Fund provides children of limited means the incredible experience of a week at Luther Heights Bible Camp in the stunning Sawtooth National Recreation Area near Ketchum, Idaho (www.lutherheights.org).

I often recall my phone conversation with Jon when I informed him that I was running for public office. "Dad, can't you find another way to make a difference?" Tragically, I have.

Linda and I and the board of the Jon Francis Foundation are committed to continuing to find ways to make a difference and pass on Jon's legacy of love and service. We strive to bring hope and help to others in a time of hopelessness and helplessness.

With courage, Jonathan David Francis transformed his faith into works. He loved bravely. Jon knew that love "bears all things, believes all things, hopes all things, endures all things." I live on, inspired by his life, and look forward, in hope, to a time when I will meet Jon on the mountaintop.

Jon Francis Foundation

The mission of the Jon Francis Foundation (JFF) is to support and empower others coping with the disappearance of a loved one, by providing hope, knowledge and resources, and to reduce incidents of loss through wilderness safety training and information.

We are guided by the belief that no human being should ever be abandoned in the wilderness. Thank you for caring and for helping others through Jon's legacy of love and service. Jon Francis Foundation is an approved Minnesota nonprofit, IRS tax exempt, 501(c) (3) corporation.

Your support is important and deeply appreciated.

www.jonfrancis.org

APPENDIX

Media Coverage

Authorities call off search for hiker

By TERRY SMITH
Express Staff Writer

Custer County authorities have called off the search for a Utah man missing since Saturday, July 15, in the Sawtooth National Recreation Area.

The search for Jon Francis, 24, a youth minister from Ogden, Utah, was suspended Tuesday evening, according to a statement from the Custer County Sheriff's Office.

"The search for Mr. Francis went as far as it possibly could go with the resources available," the sheriff's office reported. "There were ground search teams, a fixed-wing aircraft, a helicopter, and search and cadaver dogs."

A three-day search in the area of Grand Mogul near Redfish Lake south of Stanley failed to find a trace of Francis' whereabouts, the sheriff's office reported.

Meanwhile, Francis' parents,

from Stillwater, Minn., have continued the search on their own, according to the St. Paul Pioneer Press.

Francis was reported missing Sunday afternoon, July 16, after he failed to return the previous day from a planned climb up Grand Mogul.

Originally from Stillwater, Minn., Francis is a youth minister at Ascension Lutheran Church in Ogden. He has spent the last several summers as a counselor at Luther Heights Bible Camp, which is located some 40 miles north of Ketchum near Alturas Lake.

A press release from the bible camp credited searchers with working diligently to locate the missing minister:

"They worked extremely hard; their dedication and support have

JON FRANCIS

been important to all of us. It appeared that they conducted a systematic, competent and thorough search for our dear friend Jon Francis."

The Pioneer Press reported that Francis is a former cross-country runner and an experienced hiker and climber.

His father, David Francis, a state senate candidate in Minnesota, told the Pioneer Press that he thinks his son had trouble descending Grand Mogul, but is still alive.

The Pioneer Press further reported that friends and family members have been calling congressional and gubernatorial offices in Idaho and Minnesota requesting that the search for Francis be resumed.

181

Family of missing hiker not giving up

Jon Francis missing 19 days now

By DANA DUGAN
Express Staff Writer

"The search continues," David Francis said. A retired Navy captain and nuclear submarine officer, Francis, who is in the middle of a campaign for the Minnesota state Senate, sat on a shady porch with his wife, Linda, and discussed the search for his son. His Naval training was coming in handy. He held himself together almost until the end of the conversation. His wife kept very still and quiet.

Jon Francis, 24, was spending his fourth summer at the Luther Bible Camp near Alturas Lake, north of Ketchum, when he disappeared Saturday, July 15, while climbing the 9,733-foot Grand Mogul in the Sawtooth Mountains. He had been working as the director of youth ministry at Ascension Lutheran Church in Ogden, Utah.

David and Linda Francis have been staying in Stanley as guests of Jeff Clegg, who owns Redfish Lake Lodge. The Francises have three daughters, two sons-in-law and five grandchildren, all of whom are helping in the search.

"He's a man of deep faith," Francis said of his son. "As a teen, he worked at a homeless shelter for children in Minneapolis. (Afterwards) our priest said, 'Your son, Jon, has a special gift working with children.'"

A program director at Luther Bible Camp, Francis' previous three summers were as a counselor. An experienced backpacker, he led trips in the Sawtooth and the White Cloud mountains. As part of its two weeks of staff training camp, camp counselors become certified in Wilderness First Aid, along with map and compass training. Jon Francis was a former cross-country runner who often hiked alone. He has made 12 summits in the Sawtooths and White Clouds, including Thompson, Snowyside, Castle and Borah peaks, his father said.

"I've learned it's not unusual for young men to hike and climb alone," David Francis said. "Here's what we know: In his log at camp, his plan was based on the Tom Lopez book on mountaineering. He was going to be bouldering on the way up. He wrote he 'climbs for the glory of God.' He was coming down the east face. He told them he'd be back at 6 p.m. He must have gotten into trouble, maybe taken a fatal fall on Saturday. That's the most likely scenario."

As many as 150 people arrived from the Francises' home state of Minnesota; Utah, where Jon Francis lived; and other Northwestern states to help once it was announced the Idaho authorities were calling off the search Tuesday, July 18.

Francis said he made calls to political friends in Minnesota who "leveraged support with their counterparts in Idaho." Gov. Jim Risch and his wife, Vicki, met with the Francis family at Redfish Lake Lodge on Sunday, July 23.

"We've been at battle stations for two weeks," David Francis said. "I'm angry now. It's been a crash course on search and rescue. The things that needed to be done never got done. I approached the incident commander on Monday, July 17, and asked if anyone had been to the summit. No one had. I asked if we could take dogs to the summit. I was told no."

"They were very, very cautious," Linda Francis said quietly.

Meanwhile, the Francis family hired Stanley-based Sawtooth Mountain Guides to mount a private search. Co-owner Erik Leidecker climbed Grand Mogul and found Francis' log entry:

"07/15/06.   Jon Francis, LHBC (Luther Heights Bible Camp) and Ogden Utah. Climbed avalanche field to east face and east ridge. Great times bouldering! All Glory to God for the climb and the beautiful Sawtooths."

As well, Sawtooth National Recreation Area Recreation Manager Ed Cannady spent four of the five-day official search on Grand Mogul. He intended to continue searching on his own.

"For the most part, our crew and Erik's crew are the ones that spent time on the upper part of the mountain, where the greatest danger was," he said. "We looked in a thousand places but there are only 10,000 places to look. You just scour as best you can. The family was extremely gracious and strong. I was just so impressed."

At the Custer County Sheriff's Office, said the search is now "strictly on a volunteer basis," and is no longer official.

Nevertheless, it was the intervention of Risch that moved the search along last week.

Ryan Jung, one of the Sawtooth Mountain Guides, was asked to be in a helicopter by Gary Gadwa, a retired Idaho Department of Fish and Game conservation officer. Gadwa was coordinating plane flights at the request of the governor, Leidecker said.

In the air for five and a half hours on Friday, July 21, Jung said the whole thing was frustrating. "They worked with us very well. The crew engineer operated the forward-looking infrared system, known as FLIR. The screen is only 7 to 8 inches. It's good for surveillance or to stop intruders, but it doesn't work for looking in three-dimensional topography. The human eye is more sensitive to color.

"I asked if a body would show, and the crew said it wouldn't."

Leidecker spent the night of Saturday, July 29, on the mountain with a dog.

"Day by day, it's all up to the family," Liedecker said Monday. "They've discussed leaving, but, ultimately, what we do is all at their request. They want closure.

"We know the terrain and the mountains and how he climbed up and how people generally descend, but other than that we have no clues on how he came down. Our best guess is he slipped and fell but

I have no idea."

Leidecker said they have covered 50 to 60 percent of the area. "Higher probability areas have been searched by dogs."

The helicopter search covered the east ridge and northwest face, some of neighboring Mount Heyburn and the south ridge, the canyon just west of Grand Mogul called Outside Chance, Elephant's Perch and Saddle Back Lakes.

"We're very grateful to the people of Idaho. They've been so supportive with housing, meals and everything, but local and elected officials didn't want anybody injured on their watch," David Francis said. "Erik has been the best, of course, a real blessing. We needed someone to step up. The Minnesota Legislature and our friends exerted pressure on (Idaho), but they probably have limited resources. It was really a capable search. The biggest regret is that we weren't on the same team."

"We were on the same team, just not the same page," Linda Francis said. "It's been a tremendous effort."

"The critical error was not getting dogs on the summit early," Francis said. "This is a recovery effort now, I think. We continue to grieve and heal and stay engaged with the Sawtooth Mountain Guides."

On Monday, David Francis said Johnny Unser, of Sun Valley, had brought two of his search-trained dogs up to help, and there had been a possible alert from one of the other search dogs, which turned out to be false.

The last phone conversation the Francises had with their son was on Wednesday, July 12.

"He was excited about our trip out here. We were coming in August," Francis said. "He said, 'I know you miss me, but I love it out here.' I said, 'Jon it's called leaving home.'

"He was in love with the mountains."

The Francis family has a Web site—www.jonfrancis.org—devoted to up-to-date news and information on helping in the search and as a memorial.

Parents of missing rock climber aren't giving up yet

doug grow columnist

Jon Francis' mail is being routed from his home in Ogden, Utah, to his parents' home in Stillwater.

"His Blue Cross bill came," said Jon's father, David. "My wife looked at me — 'Should we pay it?'"

David knew his spouse, Linda, wasn't really asking a question. She was making a plea: Keep holding onto the hope that Jon might somehow be alive in Idaho's Sawtooth Mountains.

"Let's just pay thè bill," he said to Linda.

Late in the morning of July 15, Jon Francis reached the summit of Grand Mogul. He signed the register. "All Glory to God for the climb and the beautiful Sawtooth," the 24-year-old man wrote.

There's been nothing since.

David Francis and Jocelyn, one òf his grown daughters, returned to the mountain Thursday, this time with 20 people and specially trained dogs.

"This is about body recovery, not a search," he said before departing.

But even though every rational thought tells him his son died scrambling on the mountain's boulders, he clings to hope that somehow Jon will be found alive.

In the past few weeks, he and Linda have studied how to perform rescue operations. And they've tried to get past the anger they feel toward Idaho government officials, who they believe were too quick to declare that Jon likely was dead and that continuing a full-scale search would put others in danger.

"After one day, the sheriff told me, 'You'd better be prepared to give your son over to the mountain,'" Francis said.

Grow continues: Missing son was a champion athlete. **B2►**

Parents of missing man hold onto slim hope

◄ **GROW FROM B1**

Francis tried to explain to the sheriff that his son was in excellent shape — a runner and an experienced rock climber, not to mention a man of great spiritual depth.

After 2½ days, Francis said, the sheriff all but ended the search, despite pressure from political figures in Minnesota.

It has been up to family and friends to keep the search going.

For them, searching is easy compared with the rest of life. Searching's a focused action. Everything else is done in an awful fog.

Once in a while, Francis tries to step out of that fog. He's the DFL candidate for the state Senate seat being vacated by Michele Bachmann, and last week he participated in a parade in Lino Lakes.

A few months ago, that race seemed so important. Francis was weary of the narrow social agenda being pushed by Bachmann, now the Republican candidate for the U.S. House in the Sixth-District.

"I needed to do the parade to show my supporters that this still matters," said Francis, who is running against Ray Vandeveer.

Both Vandeveer, a conservative who is giving up his House seat for the shot at the Senate, and Bachmann have been sympathetic to Francis.

"Good people," Francis said of the two. "Politics isn't about good people and bad people, it's about ideas."

But in these awful days, he said, he won't start pushing hard in his campaign until after a celebration of Jon's life is held Sept. 9 at Ascension Episcopal Church in Stillwater.

For now, Francis wants to talk

Provided by the Francis family
Jon Francis, 24, climbed to the summit of Grand Mogul mountain in Idaho and then vanished.

about his son.

Jon Francis, a young man filled with joy. A Bible camp counselor. A youth director at a church in Ogden. A wonderful athlete. Humble.

"When he was in high school, his [Stillwater High] cross country team won the state championship and they were voted national champions," his father recalled. "Jostens created a special ring for the team, but he wouldn't buy it. I kept telling him, 'You should get one of those. You earned it. It would be something you'll always be proud of.' He told me, 'I don't need a ring. I'll carry what we did in my heart. That's enough.' He always walked humbly with God."

Now, he's somewhere on a mountain.

"It's such a big mountain," his father said.

Doug Grow • dgrow@startribune.com

Hundreds gather in Stillwater for Francis memorial

BY MARK BROUWER
Staff Writer

Hundreds gathered at Ascension Episcopal Church in Stillwater on Saturday morning to remember the life of Jon Francis.

Jon Francis

Francis, 24, had grown up in Stillwater, before attending college in South Dakota and eventually becoming a youth minister in Utah and Idaho. He disappeared on July 15 while hiking alone on Grand Mogul, a 10,000-foot peak in the Sawtooth Mountains. After months of searching, no trace of him has yet been found.

"It doesn't seem like a celebration for many of us," said the Rev. Jerry Doherty, who presided at the gathering, which was labeled in the service programs as "a celebration of a life and a ministry." "The feelings many of us bring are feelings of loss, not feelings of joy ... Jon was lost, we don't know where he is — that's the most difficult kind of grief of all," he said.

Doherty is a friend of the Francis family, has vacationed with them, and served as minister to the young man through his youth. Shortly after Francis disappeared, Doherty traveled to Utah to provide support and to aid in the search effort.

At the service, Doherty recalled the words of one searcher.

"I don't know where Jon is, I can't believe we can't find him," Doherty was told. "It's as if he were lifted off the top of the mountain."

"And that's how I prefer to think of Jon," Doherty said. "Just like Elijah was taken up by the chariots of fire, or Jesus ascended into heaven, Jon is no longer with us. ... It's the same kind of loss."

Jon's father, David Francis, admitted he was among those having trouble celebrating.

See FRANCIS, Page 4A

'Don't blame yourselves; don't blame God," said Francis' former minister

Francis 'Don't blame yourselves; don't blame God,' says Francis' former minister

Photo courtesy David and Linda Francis

For the past four summers, Francis, 24, had worked at Luther Heights Bible Camp, near Stanley, Idaho. He climbed most of the major peaks in the mountain range.

Continued from Page 1A

"We should not be here today. This should not be happening to us. Children should bury their parents," David Francis said, opening a tribute to his son. "But we are here today to celebrate the great life and ministry of Jon Francis."

The elder Francis described his son — who had attended Ascension Episcopal as a youth, was a gifted long-distance runner in both high school and college, and was pursuing a career as a Lutheran minister — "a man of strong character, deep faith, patience,

a sense of fun and adventure, and most of all unconditional love."

As David Francis told anecdotes about Jon's years growing up in Stillwater, he elicited tears, laughter — and sometimes both, from the gathered. When Jon was 8, he said, the boy demonstrated his early environmentalism by refusing to wear insect repellent containing DEET during a trip to the Boundary Waters. The result was "126 insect bites" on the boy's body.

Other stories recalled kind-

ness — such as the morning Jon Francis cheered a friend, who was dreading a morning practice, by serving him birthday cupcakes. David Francis shared also a moment of friendly rivalry, when Jon easily outdistanced him in a race and quipped "Hey, Dad. I didn't expect you back so soon."

About 600 people turned out for the service, Doherty estimated. For several blocks surrounding the North Fourth Street church, cars lined the streets. Inside, the sanctuary, and an overflow room in the parish hall were filled.

Young men wearing cross-country jackets bearing the logo of Francis' alma mater, Augustana College of Sioux Falls, S.D., attended.

Laura Aase, program director at Luther Heights Bible Camp near Stanley, Idaho, led those gathered in singing "Arms of Love," by Craig Musseau. Playing an acoustic guitar, she sang the refrain, 'My heart is glad that You've called me Your own/There's no place I'd rather be than in Your arms of love." Jon Francis frequently played the song as part of his youth ministry, his father said.

As he had in recent summers, Jon Francis had been a counselor at the Bible camp, located about 20 miles from the beginning of the climb. He also

worked several hours away as a youth minister at Ascension Lutheran Church, in Ogden, Utah.

Printed on the back of the service program was a photocopy of Jon Francis' last known words, which he wrote in a log book at the mountain's peak. "All Glory to God for the climb and the beautiful Sawtooths."

Doherty said such words were a mark of a "true believer" of Christianity, a person who is always with God. As such, Doherty urged those attending to not be angry at themselves or anyone else for Jon Francis' disappearance.

"Don't blame yourselves," Doherty said. "And don't blame God."

Jon is the son of David and Linda Francis of Stillwater. His sisters are Robin, 40, of Brooklyn, N.Y.; Jocelyn, 38, of Davis, Calif.; and Melissa, 35, of Stillwater.

The Francis family plans to conduct another search in the vicinity of Grand Mogul on Sept. 23, and are encouraging experienced climbers to join them. They ask that interested parties leave a message and their contact information at the www.jonfrancis.com web site. To date, searchers have covered most likely ascent and descent routes, but have searched only 35 to 40 percent of the area,

said David Francis.

Also, the family has established a fund to help pay for private search and rescue operations. To donate, contact The Episcopal Church of the Ascension in Stillwater at 651-439-2609 or send donations to the church at 215 N. Fourth St., Stillwater, MN 55082.

Mark Brouwer is at 651-439-4366 and at mbrouwer@stillwatercourier.com.

Above: The Francis family, Christmas 2004.

Left: Jon Francis competes in a cross-country race during his junior year at Stillwater Area High School. Francis ran on the team for five seasons, including two state championship teams.

Remembering Jon Francis

To see these and many more photographs from the life of Jon Francis, *in color,* visit the "Photo Galleries" section of the Courier's web site, www.stillwatercourier.com.

'Nothing is ended until we find him'

With their 24-year-old son still missing on an Idaho mountain, David and Linda Francis, of Stillwater, are working to help others, even as they struggle to reconcile themselves to his fate. But this summer, the family will resume their search and, they hope, bring Jon home.

STORY BY **MARY DIVINE** PHOTOS BY **JEAN PIERI** PIONEER PRESS

Linda Francis scans mall parking lots, grocery aisles and airports, looking for her lost son.

She spends hours at her computer, poring over aerial pictures of the Idaho mountains where he vanished last summer, searching for some sign, some trace of him.

And she recently was watching TV when her heart stopped: There on the screen was a young man with curly brown hair — just like Jon.

"I look every place. Everywhere," Francis says. "I'm always looking. Nothing is ended until we find him."

Jon Francis, 24, disappeared while climbing Grand Mogul in Idaho's Sawtooth Mountains last summer. His Stillwater family spent weeks at the mountain, searching and praying for him. More than 300 volunteers — strangers and friends — joined them.

SEARCHING FOR JON, 8A

(continued)

"Most likely, we know that Jon is no longer alive," says Jocelyn Francis Plass, one of his three older sisters. "But you cling to hope. We're human, you know. You cling to that little glimmer of hope, even if you know that's completely absurd. Your mind plays tricks on you. You start to think: What if this happened, or what if that happened?"

One what-if haunts them: What if they had known more about how to search in the wilderness? Would they have gotten search dogs to the summit sooner — as Jon's father, David Francis, now knows they should have?

To help other families avoid such second-guessing, the family launched the Jon Francis Foundation, which is dedicated to getting information and advice to families searching for people missing in the wild.

They were holding its first fundraiser this weekend — timed to Jon's 25th birthday, which is Monday — at Ascension Lutheran Church in Ogden, Utah, where Jon served as director of youth ministry.

Jon was last seen July 15, when he left the Luther Heights Bible Camp near Ketchum, Idaho, for a trek to Grand Mogul's 9,733-foot summit. The graduate of Augustana College in Sioux Falls, S.D., told his fellow camp counselors he would be back that evening, but he never returned. They reported him missing the next day.

The Francises rushed to Idaho and arrived at the mountain July 17. David Francis became frustrated with the official search almost immediately — when he learned no one had gone to the summit to see whether Jon had made it.

A mountain guide volunteered to go to the top of the peak and found a message from Jon: "Great times bouldering!" Jon had written in the log at the top. "All glory to God for the climb and the beautiful Sawtooths."

The Idaho law enforcement search was called off July 18. The Francises were furious.

David Francis wishes that he had been more assertive with officials.

"I should have said, 'No way in hell are you going to abandon the search after two days!'" he says. "There was a lot of unfairness in the search. Obviously if it was the sheriff's son or the governor's, they wouldn't have stopped after two days."

Says Plass: "You arrive there and, maybe it's naive, but you expect the sheriff's office to handle the search. I expected a much longer, more detailed search, but we were in no position to fight for them to do what we think they should have done."

Idaho officials rejoined the search later in the week, after volunteers began arriving — and after some political pressure. The searches proved fruitless.

Officials from the lead search agency, the Custer County sheriff's office, would not comment on the Francises' concerns about the initial search. Linda Dubiel, chief deputy, said the sheriff's office would not be involved in any further search "unless we are called to assist with a body recovery."

The Francises started to take matters into their own hands. They hired a professional searcher, who said Jon Francis was probably fit enough to survive about a week in the wilderness with a minor injury. The searcher also said that based on Jon's previous climbs, he would likely have descended the same way he climbed up — along the mountain's northeast ridge.

Veteran mountain rescue volunteer Rod Knopp called that route treacherous.

"The terrain is so steep and

rocky, it would be easy to fall," says Knopp, who is coordinator of Idaho Mountain Search and Rescue. "It's dangerous, especially for a single person without the proper equipment. On that northeast face, a slip and a fall would most likely be fatal."

Knopp said the decision to call off the official search after less than three days was not unreasonable and said every search is different.

The Francises hired private guides to navigate the rugged terrain. Doug Plass, Jon's brother-in-law, used his 3-year-old daughter's crayons to color a contour map: magenta, purple, aqua and yellow lines mark which areas were searched and when.

Family members say they kept expecting Jon to walk down off the mountain.

"I fully expected to see him walk out, looking a little rough, with a blanket wrapped around him, saying he was hungry," Jocelyn Francis Plass says.

Plass says she and her mother had the "horrific" task of making their own missing posters.

"No family should ever have to do that," she says. "I had to do it in my chicken scratch and borrow the photocopy machine at the lodge and find thumbtacks with my mother and two children in the car on a 90-plus-degree day and then drive around to the trailheads. It was gruesome. You expect somebody else to handle the details."

That's one of the goals of the Jon Francis Foundation, says Plass, who lives in Davis, Calif., and will be the group's executive director.

"I never want another family to feel hopeless ... or have to make their own missing-persons posters," she says.

Plass says the foundation's Web site — www.jonfrancis.org — aims to be a resource.

Jon Francis, 24, remains missing in the Sawtooth Mountains of Idaho

"There wasn't one source that we could go to on the Internet where we could find search-and-rescue experts," she says. "We needed information on how to get a helicopter, how to get dog teams, how to get mountaineers — people who have done this type of thing in the past — and we severely lacked the expertise."

They see a need for their work. In Idaho alone, Idaho Mountain Search and Rescue fields about 30 calls for help a year. Nationwide, there were 111 climbing accidents — 34 of which were fatalities — in 2005, according to the American Alpine Club in Golden, Colo.

"We can say: 'We've been there, done this. This is what you need to be thinking about,'" David Francis says. "We want to package and collect the knowledge that we've accumulated and pass it on to others. Pay it forward."

The foundation will also focus on wilderness-safety advice for climbers and others.

"It's pretty simple: If you have the right tools, you can be found," Linda Francis says. "We want to put simple things in the hands of hikers that they should be carrying — like a mirror and a whistle."

An experienced backpacker and climber, Jon had led climbing trips in the Sawtooth Mountains and was trained in wilderness first aid. He grew up camping and canoeing in the Boundary Waters Canoe Area Wilderness and started mountain climbing while he was a student at Stillwater Area High School.

He had reached 12 summits in the Sawtooths. People who had climbed with him told his family he was a fit and capable scrambler who didn't take chances.

But Jon made some mistakes last July: He summited a very difficult mountain by himself and didn't mark a trail, David Francis says.

The family plans to resume their search for Jon this summer. They are renting a house near the mountain and inviting friends to come and help them.

"We need to rethink the problem," David Francis says. "When we go in June, we'll search new areas that we haven't searched before. My thinking is, he's out of sight. We need to start looking at crevasses or holes on or near the summit. I guess we're driven by

two things. We want to lay him to rest; that's important. Secondly, but not nearly as important, is we want to understand what happened."

David Francis is already making preparations: He has bought a black overnight bag and packed it with a global-positioning device, walkie-talkies, a first-aid kit and a water bottle with built-in purifier. All the search information — maps, messages, phone numbers and a photo of Jon the day he disappeared — is stored in two thick three-ring binders.

The 63-year-old former Navy captain and retired businessman, who ran unsuccessfully for the Minnesota Senate last fall, is also taking a search-and-rescue class and learning to climb on an indoor climbing wall.

His training includes a two-day search-and-rescue wilderness camp in north-central Wisconsin in April.

"Given all the practical experience in the classroom, it will make me more effective and smarter out on the mountain," he says. "I was a rookie last summer. I was no help at all."

The Francises are convinced they will find Jon this summer. They are prepared to spend the summer in Idaho, but hope to be there only a week or two.

The couple has talked at length about what they will do once Jon is found. They plan to mark the area, hold a vigil and then bring his remains home to Minnesota to be cremated. They will place his ashes in the columbarium at the Cathedral of Our Merciful Savior in Faribault, where Jon was baptized.

In the meantime, Linda Francis, 63, reads Jon's books and letters he never finished. She listens to the music he liked — "U2, very loud." Her own books are stacked on the coffee table: "Touching the Edge," "Lament for a Son," "If I Could Mend Your Heart," "Ambiguous Loss."

"Touching the Edge" was written by a Minnesota woman whose son fell from Washington state's Mount Rainier, she says.

"It was the same, but not the same," she says. "They found her son, but they haven't found mine. It's draining to not know."

For David Francis, grief is physical: He says he feels a sharp pain whenever he sees other men with their sons.

He keeps a picture of Jon's first day of kindergarten in a frame on the desk of his home office. The photo, from the fall of 1987, shows father and son walking hand in hand, away from home, Jon's backpack covering his small frame.

They last talked by phone July 12 — three days before Jon disappeared. Jon told his father: "I know you miss me, but I love it out here."

David Francis replied: "Jon, it's called leaving home."

Mary Divine covers Washington County. She can be reached at mdivine@pioneerpress.com

MISSING YOU

Augustana coach runs for missing athlete, Stillwater runner Jon Francis

Reprinted with permission by Mick Garry

WHEN THE ROAD GOT TOUGH

in Sunday's Seattle Marathon, Augustana track and cross country coach Tracy Hellman glanced down at the picture of Jon Francis printed on his shirt. Francis had always been a special part of Hellman's program at Augustana. The Stillwater, Minnesota, athlete was his first recruit as head coach of the Vikings, a five-year runner within the program, and also a friend.

It was July 15 that Francis left a bible camp near Ketchum, Idaho, to climb Grand Mogul peak in the Sawtooth Mountains. The youth minister was never seen again, presumed dead on the mountain and the victim of a climbing accident, although his body has never been found. The circumstances regarding Hellman's effort in memory of Francis are heartwarming. The details regarding his former athlete's disappearance are tragic. Somewhere between, those close to Jon Francis continue to deal with the sadness of the loss.

"I tried to picture him running in the marathon," Hellman said. "The last five miles of the race there were some huge hills to deal with. I know Jon's goal was to break three hours, so it was my goal, too. I glanced down at the picture, and it gave me the motivation to keep pushing." Hellman, who finished 13th overall with a time of 2:54:19 on a cold and sloppy Seattle day, had been

asked by the Francis family to run in place of Jon, who had registered to run in the race before his disappearance.

David and Linda Francis were retrieving Jon's belongings in Ogden, Utah, where Jon was working as a youth minister at a Lutheran church. They came across his registration for the marathon and began thinking about possible ways to honor their son.

David Francis, who has also run marathons, considered running in his son's place, but aiding the search, coupled with grief and a campaign for a Minnesota state senate seat, made training impossible.

"Our daughter suggested Tracy, and she asked him if he'd be willing to run for Jon," David Francis said. "We're all doing grief work

PROFILE: JON FRANCIS   by David and Linda Francis

Home Town: Stillwater, Minnesota

High School: Stillwater, Class of 2000

College: Augustana, Sioux Falls, South Dakota, Class of 2005

Majors: Religion, Spanish and International Studies

Career Highlights: 800 meters, 2:04, 1600 meters, 4:25. 10, 3200 meters, 9:36-26. 5K, 15:58. 10K, 31:21.21. 3000 meter Steeplechase, 9:41.47. 2000 meter Steeplechase, 6:11.98. Lincoln Marathon, 3:12.54. Winner - Gopher to Badger Half Marathon (1:14.36).

Born to Run

We could see that our son, Jon Francis, was built for running when he was five years old. As a beginning soccer player, Jon was quick to the ball and would race back and forth on the field faster than anyone else.

at different paces and in different ways. We thought it was important that Jon's life be honored and recognized. This was Tracy's way of doing it."

Hellman contacted the marathon's organizers and explained the situation. He was given Jon's registration number and ran wearing a shirt with his former runner's face screen-printed on the front.

"I felt the best for a marathon I've ever felt, which is odd, because I wasn't able to train for it like I have for some of the others I've run," Hellman, a Redfield native, said. "I had bronchitis, which kept me from running for about a month. I wasn't sure how well I was going to do. I just wanted to finish for Jon."

Hellman began the race conservatively and then, when he realized he was feeling pretty good, began running harder.

"I talked with my family and friends afterward," Hellman said. "It was like Jon was watching over me."

Francis, an avid climber, was working at Luther Heights Bible Camp near Ketchum, Idaho, when he left to climb the Grand Mogul peak this summer. He made it to the top, writing "Great bouldering!" and "All glory to God for the climb and the beautiful Sawtooths" in a log registry at the summit.

There has been no sign of him since.

More than 300 people have helped in the search since then. The family has not given up, though the winter will prohibit them from searching again until May.

"I think Jon is in a place where he wants to be now, but as parents and loved ones, it's not finished until we find his remains. We want to give him a proper Christian burial in the tradition."

Included in the vain search in the first week after the disappearance was Hellman, who drove with assistant coach Chris Bradford to Idaho to help.

"It's really tough to put into words what I was feeling when I was running," Hellman said. "To be running in memory of one of my former runners, who they haven't found yet, I just can't put it into words. It's just hard to believe they had so many people on that mountain and nobody could find anything."

At www.jonfrancis.org, people can find ways to aid in the search effort. In addition, the family will start the Jon Francis Foundation in January. The organization will seek to help families put in the same position the Francis family faced during those terrible first days.

"When we arrived in Idaho on July 16, we didn't know anything about search methods, or how to organize people or raise money," David Francis said. "These are things I never wanted to know, but now I know. We want to help people who are trying to find climbers and hikers who go missing."

Information about the foundation can be found at, www.jonfrancis.org.

"Jon was such a positive instrument for Augustana's program," Hellman said. "He brought an energy to everything he did. He was a talented runner, but it was his positive outlook that was most memorable. He was the glue that held the team together." ■

Jon was born in Northfield, Minnesota, on March 5, 1982, our fourth child and our only son. The Francis family moved to Stillwater when he was eight. Jon continued to play soccer, but was drawn to competitive running as he began to realize his God given talent.

When he was a ninth grader, in Stillwater Junior High, Jon was selected for the Stillwater High School varsity track team and junior varsity cross country. When Jon entered High School in 1997, he made varsity cross country.

An Awesome Year

Jon's first year of high school varsity cross country was an awesome year. There is no other superlative than awesome that really fits. As a sophomore, Jon was the number four runner on the seven member team led by the legendary Luke Watson.

The 1997 Stillwater High School Boy's Cross Country team went undefeated. They were Conference, Section and State Champions and were voted by the sports writers as National Champions (ranked first out of 23,000 high school boy's teams).

Jon finished eighth at the Sectional, completing the 5K course in 16:18, and qualifying for his first Minnesota State Meet. At the Minnesota State High School Cross Country Running Meet, on the first weekend in November at St. Olaf College in Northfield, Jon was the 15th competitor and the fourth Stillwater runner to cross the finish line. Jon earned All Conference and All State honors that year.

This was a "three-peat" for Stillwater, their third consecutive Boy's Cross Country Championship. Local sports writers dubbed them "The Magnificent Seven." Jostens created a "super bowl style" championship ring for the team.

Jon would not order a ring. We encouraged him to buy one. But Jon said: "Dad, I don't need a ring. I know what we did." (touching his heart) he said: "I carry it in here."

Great Genetics and Great Coaching

The team's success was not just the result of hard work, talent and good genetics. It stemmed from the outstanding coaching of one of the best high school coaches in the country, Scott Christensen. Christensen's intelligent, scientific and disciplined training philosophy was a good match for Jon's speed, intensity and work ethic and helped Jon reach his highest potential as a high school athlete.

In 1998, Jon's junior year, and second year of varsity cross country, he was consistently ranked in the top 10 of high school runners, was named All-American, ran a 5K personal best of 15:58, finished second at the Sectionals and was sixth overall (fourth among team runners) at the Minnesota State High School Meet.

Jon's time of 16:02 was his personal best and the fourth fastest time for a Stillwater runner at the State Meet. Unfortunately, Stillwater placed third that year at the State Cross Country Meet in Northfield.

Off Course

In his senior year of high school cross country, Jon was elected team captain and was the last of "The Magnificent Seven" on the team. That year he made headlines at the Sectional Meet when the golf cart driver took a wrong turn. Jon was in the lead, on record pace and following the cart. When Jon realized his mistake, he and several others had taken a 200 yard detour. Jon regained the course and finished 11th.

Not finishing among the top 10 individuals meant that Jon did not qualify for the State Meet.

Jon accepted personal responsibility for the error. However, others did not, and heavily lobbied the media and The State High School League to own up to the official's mistake and to enter Jon into the 1999 State High School Meet.

It worked, and Jon ran his third and final Minnesota State High School Cross Country Running Meet as an individual competitor. One of his fans placed a sign on the road side in Northfield that read: "Welcome Home Jon."

On Track

As an outstanding middle distance track runner, Jon qualified for the State High School Track Meet and True Team for four consecutive years and is listed on the honor roll for his 3200 meter time of 9:36.26 and 1600 meter time of 4:25.10. Stillwater Boy's Track won State in 1996, 1997 and 1998 and True Team in 1997 and 2000. In 2000, Jon also finished first in the 2000 meter Steeple Chase at the 100th Annual Carleton College Invitational Track and Field Meet with a time of 6:11.98.

Off to College

Jon was heavily recruited by colleges but chose Augustana College in Sioux Falls, South Dakota, because he was attracted by the community of faith and its running coach, Tracy Hellman. We drove Jon to Sioux Falls in the fall of 2000 along with dozens of running shoes and his old, tattered "lucky" running shorts. At Augustana, Jon ran track and cross country for five years, often competing against his high school classmates, including a few of the "Magnificent Seven" from Stillwater.

Upon a
foundation, hope

Story by Mark Brouwer

Through Jon Francis Foundation, lost hiker's family seeks to heal by helping others

The Jon Francis Foundation – its goals

This winter, the Francis family of Stillwater founded the Minnesota nonprofit Jon Francis Foundation in hopes of providing for others who lose loved ones in the wilderness what they say they didn't have last summer — a place to go for help.

"The Jon Francis Foundation will act as a resource to distraught and confused individuals and families who are dealing with the disappearance of a loved one," foundation literature states. "At a time when families need to be 'at peak performance,' they are disabled with grief and sidelined by a lack of knowledge."

The families of missing climbers, hikers, hunters are among those the foundation aims to serve through a Web site "handbook" that contains information about search and rescue resources, links to groups and agencies that can offer assistance, as well as basic information about wilderness safety products and practices that can help prevent the need for rescue operations.

The foundation's mission, according to its Web site, "is to provide families with logistical and emotional support during a wilderness search and rescue operation and to

increase knowledge and awareness of wilderness safety to reduce incidents of loss."

In the short term, the foundation's directors are seeking qualified volunteers to help with the following tasks:

• Fundraising: A fundraising committee will solicit operating funds and other revenue for the foundation.

• Education: An education committee will be responsible for creating and distributing information on wilderness safety through means including wilderness safety course web content, brochures and search-and-rescue best practices.

• Product awareness: Others will identify and market safety products and/or information on safety products pertinent to wilderness safety and search and rescue.

• Search and rescue: support families and individuals coping with the loss of a loved one, missing in the wilderness, through a network of capable partners and logistical support.

• Information management: Provide information on search resources, foundation partners and organizations.

Photo by Andy Blenkush

David Francis takes a short break during a training run along County Road 12 late on the afternoon of Monday, April 16. Although long an avid runner, Francis has added rock climbing to his regimen as he and his family prepare to return to an Idaho mountain this spring to search for his son Jon, who disappeared during a climb last July 15. Jon Francis was an accomplished runner who competed in cross-country at Augustana College and at Stillwater Area High School and was a member of the latter school's 1997 national championship team. On May 5, David Francis plans to run in Ogden, Utah, at the Ascension Lutheran Church "Grace Race" at which Jon set a course record last year. This year's race will be dedicated to Jon.

When David Francis lost his son Jon to an Idaho mountain last July, he didn't know much about search and rescue operations. Now he knows more than he could ever have wanted.

Over three dizzying days, the father of four learned that Jon had gone missing during a climb near the church camp where he worked, had rushed with his family to join an official search, and then watched as that search was called off by authorities just as it seemed to be finding its feet.

In the weeks and months that followed, the Francis family exhausted its bodies and their finances in repeated, private searches of the mountain, which gave them more clues but no resolution to their ordeal.

Rather than let their bitterly earned expertise go to waste, however, the family has started a foundation so that others who lose loved ones in the wilderness have more resources, direction and hope at their ready.

The family began work on The Jon Francis Foundation after a conversation David Francis had this winter with Nancy Sabin, executive director of the Jacob Wetterling Foundation, which had assisted the Francis family by providing a lost person expert last summer. That foundation — created in the aftermath of the 1989 disappearance of St. Joseph boy Jacob Wetterling — was instrumental in the search. Sabin suggested that the Francis family "consider finding a way to bring some good out of their loss."

Particularly instrumental was Jeff Hasse, the lost person expert the Jacob Wetterling Foundation introduced to the Francis family. Hasse brought science to the search, including Global Positioning Systems and computer software and now serves as search manager and a member of the Jon Francis Foundation board.

Begun Jan. 23, and run, for now at least, out of the Francis family's Stillwater home, the Jon Francis Foundation will serve two purposes: to provide much needed money to cover costs for the search for Jon, and once he is found, to provide resources for people who lose loved ones in similar circumstances.

At first, Francis hopes the foundation's Web site will become a portal for information about mounting and maintaining search and rescue operations. Also, he hopes it will become a visible advocate for awareness about wilderness dangers.

"At first, the Web site will be very important as we try to attract attention," Francis said. Eventually, it could serve as the central hub for the foundation's activities — a place where people can learn about search and rescue and wilderness safety, and know to whom they might turn if a loved goes missing

Graphic by Ian Duvall

The Jon Francis Foundation is distributing postcards featuring this image of Jon Francis, to attract attention to their cause. Created by Francis' friend Ian Duvall, the colorful image is based on a photograph he took of Francis while Francis was driving a vanload of members of an Ogden, Utah, church youth group while they were on a trip. The phrase "All Glory to God" drawn at the bottom of the image refers to Jon's last known words, which he wrote in a log book atop the 10,000-foot Grand Mogul last July 15.

in a wilderness area.

Another project could be to work with outdoor retailers and other outlets to spread information about safety equipment, including what wilderness experts consider the "10 essential" items such as compasses, maps, mirrors, and whistles, as well as more high-tech items such as GPS units and personal locator beacons, which rescuers can track to determine a person's exact coordinates.

While the Francis family could never have wished for such a task a year ago, its ordeal has attracted a board of seven members — three from the Francis family — who are particularly well suited to creating, maintaining and publicizing an organization like the Jon Francis Foundation.

Serving as president is David Francis who, as a retired U.S. Navy Captain, nuclear submarine officer and businessman who specializes in small start-up businesses. His wife, Linda Francis, a retired office manager and former regional executive for the Girl Scouts, serves as treasurer.

The foundation's full-time executive director is their daughter, Jocelyn Plass, who has a master's degree in human performance and sports studies and has worked for non-profit organizations supporting housing and educational

opportunities for middle-and-low income people.

Other board members are Hasse, the search-and-rescue expert; James Malkowski, president of EcoVision, an environmental education consulting company; David Recker, marketing director for Cummins Power Generation and David Francis' former Navy colleague; and Sheila-Marie Untiedt, a Stillwater Township resident who served with Francis on the Stillwater Township Board.

"Part of the reason I'm doing this is to help David and his family," said Untiedt. "David is the most compelling, true person and I could not say no to him. He loves his family and his glass is half-full even under the worst of circumstances.

"So there's obviously the short term and very personal goal of raising money to support the search to find Jon," she said further. "Once he is home and buried, however, we'll have a much larger function to serve."

"It's given me a sense of purpose," David Francis said of the foundation. "And it's a chance to learn about Jon, to see him how others saw him. ... It ensures that some good will come out of his loss."

Mark Brouwer is at 651-439-4366 and at mbrouwer@stillwatercourier.com.

The search will resume, but help is needed

This spring, the Francis family of Stillwater will resume its search for their son, Jon Francis, a 24-year-old youth minister who disappeared in the Sawtooth Mountains of Idaho last July. According to Jon's father, David Francis, the family has exhausted its finances in previous searches and is seeking financial support to help them continue.

Further, the family has inaugurated a foundation in Jon's honor that will, in the short term, serve as a fundraising tool for their search and, in the long term, create a resource for others who lose loved ones in the wilderness areas.

On Saturday, May 19, at 7 p.m., the foundation will hold its Minnesota kick-off event at The Episcopal Church of the Ascension Church in Stillwater.

If you wish to contribute financially to the search, and to the mission of the foundation you may do so online at www.jonfrancis.org, in person at any Wells Fargo Bank branch, or by mail to

the Jon Francis Foundation, P.O. Box 2235, Stillwater, Minnesota 55082. Also, the foundation seeks frequent-flyer miles on airlines that travel between Minneapolis and Boise, Idaho; a boat and trailer for transporting searchers and gear in Idaho. Arcview GIS software and printing services.

To volunteer physical services, call 612-963-6772, e-mail jonfrancisfoundation@gmail.com, or contact the foundation by the address listed above. Volunteers are needed to assist in the field with searches, and supporting both a base camp and an advanced base camp by cooking, cleaning, finding provisions and hauling supplies. Anyone with access to or experience with recovery dog teams would be especially valuable, organizers said. Also needed are volunteers to assist with administration, fundraising, human resources duties and marketing.

Finding purpose in a painful loss

Jon Francis Foundation hopes to help families find loved ones lost in the wild

By ANDREW WALLMEYER
awallmeyer@acnpapers.com

STILLWATER — When rescuers called off the hunt for Jon Francis after only 19 hours, David and Linda Francis knew their search was only beginning.

Since then, the Stillwater Township couple has spent 40 days and $40,000 looking for their 24-year-old son, who was last seen heading off for a solo day hike in Idaho's Sawtooth Mountains on July 15.

So far, the only definitive sign of him searchers have turned up is a note at the summit of the 9,733-foot Grand Mogul that read, "07/15/06. Jon Francis, *LHBC (Luther Heights Bible Camp) and Ogden Utah. Climbed avalanche field to east face and east ridge. Great times bouldering! All Glory to God for the climb and the beautiful Sawtooths."

Though David Francis wishes no family would ever have to go through what his has in the last 10 months, he knows hundreds do every year. That is why he and his wife created the Jon Francis Foundation, which aims to not only bring their son home to rest but to help other families do the same for their loved ones.

The group will hold its kick-off fundraiser 7 p.m. Saturday at Ascension Episcopal Church, 214 Third St. N. in Stillwater.

"This is not a solution in search of a problem — the problem exists, but few people are aware of it," David Francis said Thursday.

He said official searches frequently end before they find the lost person, and the burden of continuing the search falls on family and friends who have no prior

See Francis, page 12

Francis

(Continued from page 1)

search and rescue experience.

"We know because we've been there, and now we're painfully aware that it happens far too often," he said. "The goal of the Jon Francis Foundation is to be there during that critical transition."

A renewed search, a new beginning

Though the foundation's long-term plan is to help others find those missing in the wilderness, David Francis said the group's top priority is still to locate his son.

"The first mission is to find Jon. I want to make that clear to everyone who connects with and contributes to the foundation," he said. Once Jon is found, the foundation's next step will be to produce a guide to help other families through the search process.

"When we do find Jon it is going to be a significant achievement in search and rescue, because it's been such a complex and difficult search," Francis said. "We will have learned a lot in the process and we're going to package that as a case study and manual for similar searches."

Beyond that, the foundation aims to create a network of wilderness search experts who local agencies can call for advice or families can call in to lead a search after the official search has ended.

Though Francis said local officials do everything they can to locate missing people, they simply lack the financial resources to continue a search when the chances of finding the subject alive are slim. Another challenge is that most searches are led by local law enforcement officials who don't necessarily have a lot of experience looking for those lost in the wild.

Photo courtesy of David Francis

2000 Stillwater Area High School graduate Jon Francis in Idaho's Sawtooth Mountains. Francis went for a solo day hike on July 15 but never returned. His family has now created a foundation to continue the search for him and help others who have lost loved ones in the wilderness.

'A long, cruel winter'

The Francis family was forced to put their search on hold last October, when the onset of winter made continued mountain treks untenable. Now that the snow has retreated, they will soon renew their hunt with the help of cadaver dogs and a small team of expert climbers.

"We believe that he had a fatal fall into a deep place and that he's out of sight, which is why he has been so difficult to find," Francis said.

The search will resume June 15, again under the leadership of Jeff Hasse, a lost-person search expert who was recommended to Francis by people at the Jacob Wetterling Foundation.

"The official search team quit after 19 hours and said, 'We can't find him. Give him up to the mountain,'" Francis recalled. "We were just left in a hopeless, helpless, desperate condition. And then we had to gather our strength and courage and wits and continue a family-led search, because after three days we weren't willing to give up."

With Hasse's help, the family has been able to develop a professional search plan that they believe will eventually locate Jon.

"That help and leadership was crucial. We were muddling through as a family, just putting people on the mountain. We did OK, but that connection got us to the point where it was an expert-led search, which makes all the difference," David Francis said.

Nancy Sabin, executive director of the Jacob Wetterling Foundation, later encouraged the family to consider starting a foundation to honor Jon's memory and help other people who find themselves in similar situations.

"What we discovered is that what happened to us happens more often than you know," David Francis said, adding that there is no other organization focused on helping find those lost in the wild.

So far, the fledging group has raised $15,000, and Francis hopes Saturday's fundraiser will bring in a lot more.

"I tend to think in search days — it's $1,000 a day to search, based on last year's effort," he said. "So we've raised 15 days of search time. And we need to do better. We need to continue raising awareness and raising money, not only for a successful search, but to pursue the mission of the foundation afterwards."

Francis believes in the mission and is confident the foundation will be successful. Aside from that, he sees it as one way his son will continue to have a positive impact on the world, even after his death.

"It's been difficult," he said. "It's been a long, cruel winter, but it has given us an opportunity to do some more search planning create and launch the foundation, which we see as a way to honor Jon, honor his memory and also bring some good out of our loss."

••••

Andrew Wallmeyer covers education and the cities of Lake Elmo, Grant and Oak Park Heights for the Gazette. He can be reached by phone at 651-796-1111. To comment on this story, visit www.stillwatergazette.com.

Hiker's remains found

Utah man went missing in Sawtooths last summer

By DANA DUGAN
Express Staff Writer

Based on remains found in a rock crevice on Grand Mogul's north face Tuesday, the family of missing hiker Jon Francis believe they have finally found their son a year after he disappeared.

"There were a couple seconds of joy, and then grief set in," said David Francis, Jon's father. "It's now positive we have found Jon's remains. They were transported off the mountain yesterday."

Francis, 24, was last seen just before reaching the summit of Grand Mogul in the Sawtooth Mountains south of Stanley on July 15, 2006. The area is approximately 55 miles north of Ketchum.

JON FRANCIS

He was the director of youth ministry at Ascension Lutheran Church in Utah, and was spending his fourth summer at the Luther Bible Camp near Alturas Lake when he went missing.

Search efforts were initiated by the Custer County Sheriff's Office the day after Francis disappeared. When official searches concluded, the family continued to scour the mountains with help from Stanley-based Sawtooth Mountain Guides. In August 2006, the family also enlisted the aid of a search manager, Jeff Hasse, president of Search, Rescue, and Recovery Resources of Minnesota. The search was called off last October due to bad weather, but resumed last month. The Francis family rented a house in Smiley Creek for the summer.

"We came for the long haul," David Francis said.

On Tuesday, July 24, human remains were found in a deep crevice at 8,248 feet by Sawtooth Mountain Guides after searchers rappelled down Grand Mogul's steep north face. They were

See FRANCIS, Page 21

Jon Francis to be laid to rest in Minnesota

Continued from Page 1

returning to camp at the base of what is known as Boy Scout Couloir. The remains were found approximately 200 yards from the camp at about 3:30 p.m., Sawtooth Mountain Guides partner Erik Leidecker said Thursday.

"It's a narrow gully at the base of a 300-foot cliff band," Liedecker said. "This area had been searched, but it was not obvious. A guide found a backpack strap. Then almost immediately they started to see remains and contents from his backpack. It was strewn through the gully that is about 300 feet long from base and 20 to 50 feet wide. We speculated he fell."

At 3:45 p.m. Tuesday, Leidecker received a call from his guides. He called the family and then Custer County Sheriff Tim Eikens. On Wednesday, July 25, Custer County Search and Rescue, Sawtooth Search and Rescue, and Idaho Mountain Search and Rescue teams set out at 9 a.m. to recover the remains under the direction of Eikens.

"It's hard to say exactly what happened," Leidecker said. "The rain may have uncovered stuff. There's active rock fall and snow at the top that's melting wet."

Sparing details, he said the way the personal items and remains were strewn about made it clear that they had moved.

"His wallet was in a plastic bag," a weary David Francis said. "They haven't found his backpack, but some of the contents were there. We're working with Tim Eikens, and he will send people back up there to find as much as he can. We'd like to find his backpack and camera. It'd be a gift to see the pictures he took."

Over the past 60 days, more than 500 searchers and 70 search dogs were on the mountain, David Francis said.

"We knew where Jon was not. We knew the next area would be the north face. It's a very difficult, rugged area," he said. "One of the keys, and something important that we've learned, is to profile the

> "We knew where Jon was not. We knew the next area would be the north face."
>
> **David Francis**
> Jon Francis' father

climber. What came out was Jon had a preference for descending down gullies."

Leidecker gave a lot of credit to Jeff Hasse for his profiling work.

"He did a lot to recreate what might have happened," Leidecker said. "The reality is no one would have been there if it wasn't for Jeff and his work and the dedication of the family. They always believed he was up there. The Sawtooth Mountain Guides were involved from the first, and obviously our deepest sympathies go out to the family.

"Of course, it's also a sense of relief that he was found. A lot of guides put a lot of time in looking. The last few days have been pretty emotional for all of the

people involved. The guides who found him are the same guides who were involved since last July. From the perspective of the guides, the greatest satisfaction comes from knowing the family has closure."

David Francis said his family will stay in Idaho until all the remains have been recovered.

"Eventually, we'll lay him to rest back in Minnesota," he said. The Francis family founded the Jon Francis Foundation in early 2007 to help others with search and rescue efforts and to educate climbers and hikers about wilderness safety.

"We're serious and hopeful the foundation will be successful. There is a lot we've learned that we hope to pass on to the wilderness community. We also have discovered what a wonderful person Jon was. He made a difference in peoples' lives. We want to make a difference, just as he did."

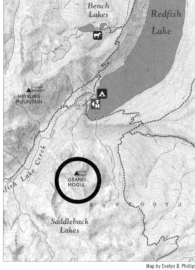

Map by Evelyn B. Phillips
Grand Mogul, where Jon Francis was hiking in July 2006 when he went missing, hovers high over the south end of Redfish Lake in the Sawtooth Mountains.

Family and friends filled a local church to remember 24-year-old Jon Francis and honor his love of the natural world, where he died 15 months ago while mountain climbing.

David Francis carries the ashes of his son, Jon, from Stillwater's Episcopal Church of the Ascension on Tuesday afternoon following services for the 24-year-old, who died while mountain climbing in Idaho in July 2006. His remains finally were recovered this summer. Jon Francis' godparents, John and Coralie Hunter, follow David Francis down the church steps.

'Jon saw God in all creation and knew it was all good'

BY MARY DIVINE
Pioneer Press

On Tuesday, David and Linda Francis added another anniversary to a lengthy calendar of mourning.

The Stillwater couple each year will mark their son Jon's birthday; the day he disappeared while climbing in Idaho's Sawtooth Mountains and the day two mountain guides found his body on Grand Mogul Mountain, about 1,300 feet below the summit he had climbed.

And now, Oct. 9 will be remembered as the day they buried their son's ashes in Stillwater Township's Historic Rutherford Cemetery under a steel-gray sky.

Friends, family members and even a search-and-rescue dog packed the Episcopal Church of the Ascension in Stillwater on Tuesday afternoon to say goodbye to Jon, bringing some closure to an ordeal that began almost 15 months ago.

Jon, 24, disappeared in the Sawtooth Mountains on July 15, 2006. After a lengthy search involving hundreds of volunteers,

CLIMBER'S FUNERAL, 10B

David Francis kept a photo of his son on a notebook containing information about the search efforts.

Climber's funeral

(continued from Page 1B)

his body was found more than a year later, on July 24. It is believed he died as the result of a fall.

The Celtic funeral honored Jon's Irish heritage and focused on his love of nature and God. The Celts believed God was in everything, said the Rev. Dr. Jerry Doherty.

"In a way, Jon is part of creation now," Doherty said. "Every time you see the sun rise, the moon coming up over the water, the leaves changing in the fall and new flowers in the spring, just as surely you're seeing Jon."

Doherty said Jon especially loved being in the mountains and died doing something he loved. He quoted the last note Jon ever wrote, the message he left in a log book on the mountain's summit: "Great times bouldering! ... All glory to God for the climb and the beautiful Sawtooths."

At the time he disappeared, Jon was working at Luther Heights Bible Camp near Ketchum, Idaho. He also was a youth minister in Ogden, Utah. Jon was majoring in reli-

gion at Augustana College in Sioux Falls, S.D., and had planned to go to seminary to become a minister.

"Jon saw God in all creation and knew it was all good," said David Francis, Jon's father. "He had a passion for others. He was full of love for others."

David Francis read part of a paper that Jon wrote for a religion class at Augustana.

"I do not know why, but I am closer to God when I am outside," Jon had written. "... I give glory to God for her abundant creation. There is goodness all round. There is goodness deep within."

The service began with a reading from Isaiah 55: "You will go out in joy and be led forth in peace, the mountains and hills will burst into song before you, and all the trees of the field will clap their hands."

It ended with David Francis accompanying his wife, Linda, and their three daughters, Robin Francis, Jocelyn Plass and Melissa Runkel, and their families from the church.

Tears filled his eyes as he cradled in his arms a simple wooden box containing his son's ashes.

Mary Divine can be reached at mdivine@pioneerpress.com or 651-228-5443.

Paying Tribute: The Jon Francis Half-Marathon

LIFE FOR THE DAVID AND LINDA FRANCIS family the past three years could be likened to a marathon.

The race, as it were, began with a phone call David received on July 16, 2006, informing him that he and Linda's only son, Jon, had gone missing after reaching the summit of Grand Mogul in Idaho's Sawtooth Mountains. The Francis family hit the first incline soon afterward when the local sheriff and the posse called off the search after only 29 hours.

"They told me, 'You need to give up your son up to the mountain,'" David recalled. Jon's parents and his three older sisters, Robin, Jocelyn and Melissa, refused. Over the course of the next year, they organized and funded their own search and rescue teams, which eventually led to the discovery of Jon's remains on July 24, 2007.

"It was grief and despair and loss all over again," David admitted.

Support and Celebration

The Francis family created the Jon Francis Foundation (www.jonfrancis.org) that year. The foundation's mission is to "support and empower others, coping with the disappearance of a loved one, by providing hope, knowledge and resources, and to reduce incidents of loss through wilderness safety training and information."

Over the past two years, the foundation has assisted several families in their search for their missing children. For David and his family, this portion of their marathon has been a journey of discovery as they have met hundreds of people whose lives Jon touched in his brief 24 years.

Another purpose for creating the foundation, David said, is to find opportunities to celebrate Jon's life. "We don't want the world to forget Jon Francis," he said.

That is why the Francis family was so excited when Stillwater Marathon Director Dave Eckberg agreed to dedicate the half-marathon in Jon's memory.

"The feeling we have as a family is intense gratitude to the community — from Dave Eckberg, to the local city councils, to the merchants, runners and volunteers — for the recognition," David said.

'I Carry It in Here'

It was a full life in many respects. Jon first made a name for himself as a high school distance runner at Stillwater Area High School. As a sophomore, he was a member of the school's undefeated state championship cross-country team, which finished the season ranked No. 1 nationally by USA Today.

Following that season, Josten's designed commemorative rings for the team (it was their third consecutive state championship). Jon, however, didn't order one. His reason exemplified the selfishness that marked his life. Said David Francis: "One day I asked him why he didn't want to order a ring for himself, and he put his hand over his heart and said, 'Dad, I know what we did -- I carry it in here. I don't need a ring to remind me.'"

Two years later, Jon turned down NCAA Division I scholarship offers, deciding instead to compete for Division II Augustana College in Sioux Falls, S.D.

A Life Devoted to Others

But Jon made a name for himself well beyond athletics. During his years at Augustana, and even after he graduated from there in 2005, Jon volunteered as a counselor at Luther Heights Bible Camp near Ketchum, Idaho. His first job out of college was director of youth ministry at Ascension Lutheran Church in Ogden, Utah. From his high school years and beyond, he volunteered for Habitat for Humanity, was a leader at Teens Encounter Christ, worked at

On a flat road runs the well-train'd runner. He is lean and sinewy with muscular legs. He is thinly clothed, he leans forward as he runs, with lightly closed fists and arms partially rais'd.
-The Runner by Walt Whitman

Gethsemane Day Camp in Minneapolis (a homeless shelter for children), led a Bible study class at Augustana and worked as a volunteer at Ascension Lutheran's preschool.

With the creation of the Jon Francis Half-Marathon this weekend, approximately five dozen friends and family members are carrying on Jon's legacy by volunteering to help staff the race course. In the process, they are raising money for the Jon Francis Foundation.

"We are excited," Jon's father said. "This race will be an event that celebrates Jon's life."

CITATION ACKNOWLEDGEMENTS

Private correspondence of Laura Aase, Caryl Bauwans, Carren Corcoran, Kevin Doe, The Reverend Jerry Doherty, Linda Francis, Robin Francis, Michael Goodwin, Bill Hall, Jeff Hasse, The Right Reverend James L. Jelinek, The Reverend M. David Kiel, Erik Leidecker, Alexis Marie Nelson, Jocelyn Plass, Melissa Runkel, and The Reverend LeeAnne Watkins. Used with permission.

Oh, the Places You'll Go! by Dr. Seuss, Random House, 1990. Reprinted with permission.

Lament for a Son by Nicholas Wolterstorff, William B. Eerdmans Publishing Company, 1987. Reprinted with permission.

"Biodance," *Stars in Your Bones: Emerging Signposts on Our Spiritual Journeys*, Alla Bozarth, Julia Barkley and Terri Hawthorne, North Star Press of St. Cloud, 1990. Used with permission.

This Mortal Marriage: Poems of Love, Lament and Praise, Alla Renée Bozarth, iUniverse, 2003. Used with permission.

Idaho: Climbs, Scrambles, and Hikes by Tom Lopez, Mountaineers Books, 2000. Reprinted with permission.

Pilgrim at Tinker Creek by Annie Dillard, HarperCollins Publishers, 1974. Reprinted with permission.

"Authorities call off search for hiker" by Terry Smith, *Idaho Mountain Express*, July 19, 2006. Reprinted with permission.

"Senate hopeful's son is missing" by Megan Boldt, *Pioneer Press*, July 19, 2006. Reprinted with permission.

"Family of missing hiker not giving up" by Dana Dugan, *Idaho Mountain Express*, August 3, 2006. Reprinted with permission.

"Parents of Missing Rock Climber Aren't Giving Up Yet" by Doug Grow, *Star Tribune*, August 27, 2006. Reprinted with permission.

"Hundreds gather in Stillwater for Francis memorial" by Mark Brouwer, *Stillwater Courier*, September 14, 2006.

"Nothing is ended until we find him" by Mary Divine, *Pioneer Press*, March 4, 2007. Reprinted with permission.

"Upon a foundation, hope" by Mark Brouwer, *Stillwater Courier*, April 19, 2007. Reprinted with permission.

"Missing You," *RunMinnesota*, March/April 2007, Edina, MN. Reprinted with permission.

"Finding purpose in a painful loss" by Andrew Wallmeyer, *Stillwater Gazette*, May 18, 2007. Reprinted with permission.

"Hiker's remains found" by Dana Dugan, *Idaho Mountain Express*, July 27, 2007. Reprinted with permission.

"Jon saw God in all creation and knew it was all good" by Mary Divine, *Pioneer Press*, October 10, 2007. Reprinted with permission.

"Paying Tribute: The Jon Francis Half-Marathon" by John Gillstrom, *Official Stillwater Marathon Runner and Spectator Guide*, May 24, 2009. Reprinted with permission.

AUTHOR ACKNOWLEDGEMENTS

The search for Jon Francis involved hundreds of dedicated and self-less volunteers. I have so many people to thank for their support and commitment.

Thank-you dinners, letters, and cards were inadequate to express the immense gratitude the Francis family felt for the many acts of courage, care, and kindness from those who joined in the search for Jon and supported us in our grief, loss, and hope.

My deepest appreciation to all who went on the mountain or who watched, waited, and prayed with us or contributed in any way to this enormous effort. In my confusion or fog of grief, I may have inadvertently overlooked some people or neglected to express my sincere thanks to some of the generous people who were with us. I was not always clearheaded or aware of all aspects of the search, so I also apologize for any inaccuracies in my records.

MY DEEPEST THANKS...

TO THOSE INVOLVED IN THE "OFFICIAL SEARCH," JULY16-18, 2006.

Custer County Search and Rescue & Sawtooth Search and Rescue

Jaimie Cannady, Jamie Clegg, Nick Dolja, Gary Gadwa, Luanna Gunderson, Tawny Hancock, Steve Herret, Cindy Hillemeyer, Pete Isner, Steve Kingslein, Levi Krope, Amanda Matthews, Steve Rogers, Sean Peterson, Casey Rotgaert, and Mike Talbot.

Blaine County Search and Rescue
Cam Dagget with canine Rocky; Johnny Unser, Jr. with canines Taz and Chili Dog.

U.S. Forest Service
Ed Cannady, Cory Cann, Greg Dusic, Joe Harper, Corey Shanahan, Kip Watson, Forest Service Helicopter Pilot Chris Templeton, and Sawtooth Helitack.

Sawtooth Mountain Guides
Kirk Bachman, Erik Leidecker, and Ryan Jung.

Treasure Valley Search Dogs, Boise, Idaho
Paula McCollum with canine Jeb, Susan Janz and Candy Krueger with canine Suzie.

To family, friends, and volunteer searchers, July 19, 2006- September 16, 2007.

The Sawtooth Mountain Guides
Tim Ball, Bozo Cardozo, Drew Daly, Marc Hanselman, Ryan Jung, Lincoln McNulty, Josh Nielsen, and Pete Patterson, under the leadership of Erik Leidecker. Thank you for your courage and commitment.

U.S. Forest Service
Ed Cannady and Greg Dusic.

Search, Rescue, and Recovery Resources of Minnesota
Jeff Hasse and Ken Anderson. Thank you for your leadership, skill, and persistence.

VOLUNTEERS FROM ACROSS THE COUNTRY

Arizona
Robert and Eileen Bower.

California
Gary Buchanan, Brian Friedrich, Michelle Fulton, John Gerber, John Kochendorfer, Steve Sterling, Scott Stranzl.

Colorado
Craig Binkley, Matt Thelen.

Florida
Danny Ibison and canine Tyler, Brian Murphy, Bill Stewart.

Idaho
Vicki Armbruster, Brian and Laura Boyd, The Bauwens (Caryl, Gay and Tom), Rob Beck, Tammy Bowerman, Tim Carver, Jordan and Heather Dale, Sean Duffy, Chris Edwards, Rick Fahey, Wayne and Sue Frieders, Bart Green, Don Green, Jordan King, Peter Madsen, Justin Malek, Ben McCoy, Gary McVann, Del and Irene Myers, Eric Olsen, Dan Rieke, Tom Rybus, Courtney Samway, Steve Stranzl, Rick Warner, Annie Williams.

Redfish Lake Lodge Owners and Staff
Jeff and Audra Clegg, Jo Jo Fuller, Hannah Marx, and Greta Rybus.

Mountain Village Lodge, Stanley
Ken and Deb Nadue.

Treasure Valley Search Dogs, Boise
Paula McCollum with canine Jeb, Susan Janz with canine Suzie.

Forensic Dogs of Idaho, Boise
Ann Moser and canine Watson.

Marlies Stroes with canine China, our neighbor from Sawtooth City.

Johnny Unser, Jr., with canines Taz and Chili Dog from Sun Valley.

Idaho Mountain Search and Rescue Unit
July 25, 2007: Tim Henning, Wade Kimball, Bill Lindenau, Bob Meredith, Dominick Merrell, Owen Miller, Rick Thompson.

September 14-16, 2007: Danny Cone, Aimee Hastrider, Bob Meredith, Owen Miller, Josh Nichols, Phil Sanders, Eric Zuber.

Illinois
Chad Backsen.

Iowa
Emergency K-9 Operation, Inc.
Bill and Lois Hall with canines Hawk and Trax.

Kansas
Nora Johnson.

Massachusetts
The Bravo family: Sam, Steve, and Stephanie.

Minnesota
Phil Alban, Tom and Nancy Austin, Jan Hogle, Jerry Doherty, John and Colleen Hooley, The Ghere's (David, Chris, Erin and Gail), Joe Paulis, Dave Recker, Jeremy Schultz.

Jacob Wetterling Resource Center (JWRC)—Nancy Sabin, Jerry and Patty Wetterling.

Montana
Ron Boswell, with canine Mahto and Twila York with canine Kona from Big Sky Search Dogs, Bill and Pam Dooley.

Nevada
Tom Ryan and canine Zorro.

New Hampshire
The Beaton family: Alyssa, Charley, Courtney, Laura, Michael, Shane.

New York
Ryan Willemsen.

Oregon
Karen Marcotte and canine Barry, Bend, Oregon; Andy Smith.

Pennsylvania
Chuck Wooters and canine Falco.

South Dakota
Chris Bradford, Andrew Ellsworth, Jim Hanley and canine Shania, Tracy Hellman, Chris Lehrer, Sven Lerseth, Chris McClurg, Paula Wheeler.

Utah
Brent Hinsley, Al Jones, and Paul Olsen.

The Mighty Ascension Search Team, Ascension Lutheran church, Ogden, Utah
>   David and Beth Borchert, Eric and Bruce Engelby, Chip Fuller, Dale Ostlie, Mike Otto, Calvin and Diana Schalk, Ken Schulte, Diane and Stuart Schultz, Jeff Turner, Larry and Cecilia West, Roy West, Joanna Wolf.

Vermont
Tim Hansen, Paul and Diana Jameson, Rusty Japikse.

Virginia
Ken Briggs.

Washington
Daniel Foregger, Scott Foster, Lee Titus, Brian Hoots, Paul Huppert, Ralph Katieb, Damon McBrinn, and Alexis Nelson.

Andy Rebman of K-9 Specialty Search Associates in Kent, Washington.

Wisconsin
Carren Corcoran with canine Cleo from Canine Search Solutions, Josh and Erica Klaetsch, the Reidt family—Brandon, Dave, and Justin.

Nicolet Search Team, Mountain, Wisconsin (instructors)
Chuck and Janine Keuhn, Deb Seline.

Wyoming
Joanie Thelen.

High Country Search Dogs and Wyoming K9 SAR, Jackson Hole, Wyoming
Sara Griffel-Thomson and canine Jenny, Chuck Schneebeck and canine Buster, Mary Shouf with canine Sofie, Ray Shriver and canine Kita, Craig Stagg, Tom Thompson, Janet Wilts with canine Chay-da.

Curt and Cathy Orde and canine Moose from Centennial, Wyoming.

Board of Directors, Jon Francis Foundation
Dave Recker, a friend, mentor, fellow retired Navy captain, and marketing executive; Sheila-Marie Untiedt, fellow town board supervisor and small business entrepreneur; Jim Malkowski, teacher and entrepreneur; John Aasan, friend, former teammate at IBM, and a sales executive; and, finally, Jeff Hasse, paramedic and search expert.

To the Francis for Senate Campaign Staff and Parade Unit, thank you for walking with me on the campaign trail.
Al and Carol Anderson; Jeanne Anderson; Alex, Eric, Nancy, and Tom Austin; John and Pat Barrett; Brian and Jerry Beedle; Margaret Boettcher; John and Karen Bower; Mark and Merrily Brandt; Chris and Karl Bremer; Jerry and Meg Castle; Mary Cecconi, Dwight and Becky Cummins; Cindy Dina; Jerry and Sheila Doherty; Mark and Brenda Doneux; Kevin and Molly Donovan; Bill Eggers; Linda and Robin Francis; Katie Gabrick; Anne and Pat Gabriel; Marty Gerkey; Nancy Gertner; David and Gail Ghere; Jason Gonnion; David and Cindy Green; Bill Haring; Jim Hunt; John and Coralie Hunter; George and Susan Johnson; Senator Steve Kelley; Mike Kennedy; Ed Kimball; Sara Kloek; Allison and Chris Kohtz; Senator Jane Krentz; Jeanine Krumpelmann; David and Joanne Laird; Deb Lauer; Mary Jane Lavigne; Jeff and Pam Ledermann; Eric and Kim Lillyblad; Chris, Heidi, Nate, Katie, and Joe Lottsfeldt; Jim and Nancy Malkowski; Terry and Jayne Marshall; Brook Martin; Pat and Jeanne Martin; Meg McConnell; Jon and Michelle Michels; Alissa, Drinda, and Greg Miller; Don Mitchell; Senator Mee Moua; Tom and Sian Nacey; Sig Nordskog; Janet O'Connell; Hope Olson; Rebecca Otto; Tom and Dianne Polasik; Dan and Linda Powell; Sandy Probst; Paul and Peg Quinn; Kim and Rob Rapheal; Jen and Rob Renzaglia; Senator Ann Rest; Melissa, Steve, Stevie, and Taylor Runkel; Bob Schmitz; Amy and Mark Schwantes; Miriam Simmons; Barb Staub; Ted Thomson; Carol Trombley; David Truax; Vivian Votava; Tom and Zantha Warth; Val and Corrine Watson; Rick and Donna Wente, Patty Wetterling; Jim and Nancy Whipkey; J.D. Wichser; Susanne Wissink; Joe Wolfe; and Nichelle Zimmer.

To those in the media, thank you for telling others about Jon's life, loss, and legacy.

Adam Atchison and Alyson Outen, KTVB, Channel 7 in Boise; Glen Barbour, KSTP, Channel 5, St. Paul; Megan Boldt and Mary Divine, *Pioneer Press*; Mark Brouwer, *Stillwater Courier*; Nate Carlyle, *Salt Lake City Tribune*; Mark Daly, KARE 11, Minneapolis; Michelle DeGrand, Channel 2, KBCI, Boise; Dana Dugan and Terry Smith, *Idaho Mountain Express*; Tom Ford, Kevin Giles, Doug Grow, and Myron Metcalf, Minneapolis *Star Tribune*; Mick Garry, *Sioux Falls Argus Leader*; Stuart Groskreutz, Kris Janisch and Andy Wallmeyer of the *Stillwater Gazette*; Jill Kuraitis, NewWest.Net/Boise; Heidi Keller Miler, *RunMinnesota*; Steve Murphy and Pat Miles from WCCO, Channel 4, Minneapolis; Bill Roberts, *Idaho Statesman*, Boise; Rebecca Palmer of the Ogden *Standard Examiner*; and Chris Williams, *Associated Press*.

Thanks to all who read my manuscript and offered help, advice, and insight.
Jill Breckenridge, Mark Brouwer, Spike Carlsen, Marly Cornell, Jerry Doherty, Doug Grow, Erik Leidecker, Chuck Logan, Nancy Raeburn, Ken Schulte, and Dave Wood.

With gratitude to my family...
Linda, you remained my strong partner throughout this difficult time and I am forever grateful for your love, patience, and encouragement.

My daughters and grandchildren: Robin, Jocelyn, Audrey, Charlie, Melissa, Taylor, Katie, and Stephen. Thank you for being a comfort in our brokenness.

My sons-in-law Doug Plass and Steve Runkel. Thank you for being at my side during our desperate search. You were awesome.

To Jon. You were with me for only a fleeting moment. But in that time, you made a difference. Thank you for being my son, friend, and inspiration. You were a gift to me from God.

ABOUT THE AUTHOR

David is a retired businessman, former nuclear submarine officer, and U.S. Navy captain with thirty years of naval service. He is also founder and president of the Jon Francis Foundation (JFF) created in 2007 to "mold our sorrow into purpose." JFF passes on Jon's legacy of love and service by helping others who are distraught and overwhelmed while coping with the disappearance of a loved one.

In addition to their son Jon, David and Linda Francis have three daughters—Robin, Jocelyn, and Melissa—and six grandchildren—Taylor, Katie, Stephen, Audrey, Charlie, and Camille. David and Linda live in Stillwater, Minnesota.